Till Death Do Us Part

A Minister's Guide to Officiating at Funeral Services

By

Jeff Moore

D.Min

CROSSBOOKS
PUBLISHING

CrossBooks™
A Division of LifeWay
1663 Liberty Drive
Bloomington, IN 47403
www.crossbooks.com
Phone: 1-866-879-0502

© 2011 Jeff Moore. All rights reserved.

No part of this book may be reproduced, stored in a retrieval system, or transmitted by any means without the written permission of the author.

First published by CrossBooks 11/21/2011

ISBN: 978-1-4627-1246-5 (e)
ISBN: 978-1-4627-1231-1 (hc)
ISBN: 978-1-4627-1232-8 (sc)

Library of Congress Control Number: 2011961469

Printed in the United States of America

This book is printed on acid-free paper.

Any people depicted in stock imagery provided by Thinkstock are models, and such images are being used for illustrative purposes only.

Certain stock imagery © Thinkstock.

Because of the dynamic nature of the Internet, any web addresses or links contained in this book may have changed since publication and may no longer be valid. The views expressed in this work are solely those of the author and do not necessarily reflect the views of the publisher, and the publisher hereby disclaims any responsibility for them.

To Mom, who taught me a great deal through her life and through her death.

Contents

Introduction 1

Chapter 1: Guidelines for Making Funeral Arrangements 3

Chapter 2: Guidelines for Conducting Funerals 9

Chapter 3: Early Encounters with Death 15

Chapter 4: Mom's Story 19

Chapter 5: Reaching Out through Funerals 25

Chapter 6: Location of the Dead in Christ 27

Chapter 7: Difficult Funerals 33

Chapter 8: The Candid Camera Funeral 41

Chapter 9: African Funeral 47

Chapter 10: Sermon Outlines with Notes 53

Chapter 11: Follow Up 103

Suggested Resources 107

Introduction

There is a great scene in the movie *Indiana Jones and the Temple of Doom* where the hero of the film, Indiana Jones, and his sidekick, Shortround, are trapped in an ancient death device filled with spikes, crushing stones, and the remains of other poor victims. Dr. Jones has the opportunity to speak to his leading lady through an opening in the wall of the death chamber. The camera focuses on Harrison Ford's distressed face as he proclaims emphatically, "We are going to die!"

These words need to sink into the hearts and minds of all of us as we look at our lives. Barring the second coming of Jesus, every one of us will die. I don't like that fact, but it is reality.

Why another book on death? I have no idea except to say that I felt led to write down some of the unique experiences of my life while dealing with funerals and death. I know there are pastors who have done more funerals than I have, and there are those who will never do the number of funerals I do. It is not a contest; in fact, I would be quick to say that I hope I never have to do another one the rest of my ministry.

My prayer is that you might find some challenges, encouragement, and maybe even a laugh or two as you read through this work. It is not my intention to embarrass, humiliate, or disrespect anyone's memory. I promise that all of the stories are true; you can't make this stuff up. If this book never sells a single copy, I will not be disappointed. My conviction was to write it. If God wants others to read it, fine. As I looked at a popular Christian book dealer online and found many similar works, the Lord had to remind me that my task was to write and leave the results up to Him.

The bulk of this work was done during a time of personal leave from my church. I am grateful for the self-improvement time my church gives me. I found a wonderful Christian retreat center in Beulah, Colorado, called the Yoke Is Easy Ranch. It is so beautiful there that I felt a strong sense of God's presence in those glorious mountains.

One more thought in this introduction: live a godly, decent life so your minister will have something to work with at your funeral. You have no idea how hard it is to say something nice at the funeral of someone who lived his life in sinfulness and separation from God and his fellow man.

I have included some sermon outlines in an effort to help anyone who may need to officiate a funeral service. I hope other ministers will benefit from the outlines or thoughts presented. Anyone called upon to share at a funeral service is welcome to rewrite the material as needed.

Guidelines for Making Funeral Arrangements

Much of this book is directed toward those who will conduct the funeral. You may have picked up this work as someone looking for answers on what to do as you plan the funeral service for your loved one. It is quite different on the other side of the pulpit. As a professional, I deal with death and funerals on a regular basis. I have only had to deal with death a few times on the other side.

I believe it is helpful for people to make arrangements ahead of time. If you can afford it, you should go to the funeral home of your choice and do as much as you can for your own funeral. This may seem morbid to some, but the truth is we are all destined to die until Jesus comes again. Your investment of time, emotion, and energy can become one of the greatest gifts you will ever give your family. Upon your death, they will encounter the painful task of making arrangements with great relief when they find you have already taken care of most of the groundwork already.

Unfortunately, only a few of us enjoy the blessing of a prearranged funeral service, so more often, the task falls squarely on the shoulders of the departed person's loved ones. You must remember that a funeral is for the living and not the deceased. This may be upsetting to you, but a funeral service is powerless to change the eternal destiny of those who have already died. Funerals are intended to comfort the grieving and honor the one who passed away.

How do you begin to tackle this hard task? Your local funeral director can provide a wealth of experience and knowledge for you. Don't be afraid to ask questions. Write down your questions and concerns as they come to mind. You have enough to think about in the midst of your grief. Don't be embarrassed by making a list of your concerns. A word of caution here: you can be overwhelmed with well-meaning people desiring to help you. Seek out those you trust and respect, and don't be afraid to make your own decisions. People have a strong desire to help during the grieving process, but sometimes the help you receive is not the help you truly need.

You will be faced with many issues as you go to make the arrangements. One of the first considerations is the time and location of the memorial service. Most tend to fall either mid-morning or mid-afternoon. You will need to decide on what day you want to have the service. Most funeral homes and churches prefer not to schedule funerals on the weekends. Funeral directors don't like to work then because they have families and personal activities, just like everyone else. Some will charge you extra for having a weekend service, so if you are insistent on holding your loved one's funeral on the weekend, be sure to ask if there is an additional charge.

Churches do not like to have funerals on Sundays because they interrupt the flow of normal activities. The custodians will have to work extra to clean the worship center after the morning service. There is also the issue of unlocking the building and making sure the heating or air conditioning is set properly for the service. If the church has evening services, there is the issue of clearing everyone out in time for the evening worship. It is also very hard on the minister to add another duty to his busiest day of the week.

You will also face the task of picking out a casket. There are a variety of materials and styles of caskets. It will likely come down to the issue of how much money you want to spend. There is no right or wrong answer when it comes to this issue; it is simply a matter of taste. Some local laws require a vault in which the casket will rest. Vaults usually range from simple concrete structures to more elaborate ones made of different materials. As with the caskets, the difference in the materials will have a related increase in price. Typically there is a grave-opening fee that simply pays someone to take a piece of heavy equipment, such as a backhoe, and dig the hole into which the casket and vault will be placed. The funeral director typically takes care of making these arrangements, but you will be required to pay the fee.

There is a question of where to have the actual funeral service. Most funeral homes have a chapel in which to conduct the service; however, many people want to hold the memorial at their local church. If this is the case, the people at the funeral home will contact the local church to set the time and date. You may be invited by the local church to have a lunch on the day of the funeral. If you choose a morning service, lunch will follow. If you have an afternoon funeral, you will have lunch prior to the service. The church will want an estimate of the number of people who might attend the luncheon. Typically the goal is to provide the meal for family and not all the guests; however, some people want to invite special friends to eat with them, which is fine. The main concern is to allow the local church the opportunity to prepare enough food for all who will attend.

Once you pick out the casket and arrange the time and place, you will have to make decisions concerning the actual service. You will need to choose pallbearers, who will be responsible for carrying the casket as a part of the service. You will need to choose someone to officiate the funeral. Usually this is the local pastor of the church.

The funeral director will need to have biographical information about your loved one. This usually includes time and place of birth, parents' and family members' names, career history, military service, church involvement, favorite activities, and the names of immediate family members who have passed away prior to your loved one.

Songs tend to be one of the more difficult areas of the decision-making process. Remember that songs typically last for three to five minutes. If you have several songs in the flow of the service, it will take several minutes. Keep in mind that there is usually a time to read the biographical information about your loved one, a message or sermon by the pastor, and perhaps a eulogy from a member of the family or friend. The longest funeral services are often the ones with the most songs.

There is a growing popularity in asking family members or close friends to stand up and share thoughts about the person who has passed away. Be aware that most people are not accustomed to public speaking, so they have no concept of time as they speak. Some will keep their comments very brief, while others may talk for ten or fifteen minutes. Nervousness can manifest itself in brevity or longevity, depending on the nature of the individual speaking. You need to take into consideration the lives and busy schedules of people who attend your family member's memorial service. A funeral can last one hour and provide adequate time for all the necessary elements; however, many services last less than an hour.

If you choose to have a local minister to preside over the funeral, you can help him by sharing any information you can about your loved one's church involvement, favorite passage of Scripture, and any special memories you feel should be shared with the congregation. Don't be embarrassed if you cannot think of any special verses of the Bible. Be willing to allow the minister to develop an appropriate message for the service.

It is likely that you will be asked if you want to open the casket at the close of the service. Sometimes this is not a consideration depending on the circumstances of death. For example, those killed in car accidents often suffer such damage and bruising to the body that it is impractical to view the corpse. People who die in fires and those whose bodies were not discovered until decay has set in also present a problem with opening the casket for public viewing. Some argue for the importance of opening the casket and others argue for the importance of not viewing the body. You must make this choice as you think best, for it is truly your decision.

I personally think it is important for family members to see the body of their loved one, even if there is disfigurement or decay. I believe, while it is difficult, it helps with the grieving process by making the death more real. If you choose to open the casket at the close of the service, be prepared for a long wait, because it takes time to file people by the casket. It will add time to the overall length of the service. Some families choose to keep the casket open prior to the beginning of the funeral service so people may view the body if they so choose. Some want the casket open before and after the service, whereas, some will even choose to leave it open for the entire service.

I have often been asked about the issue of cremation. There is nothing, to my knowledge, in the Bible to address this question directly. I personally believe that God is able to resurrect human bodies from fire, drowning, decay, or any other set of circumstances; therefore, cremation is a matter of personal choice and preference.

You will also face a decision about a tombstone or marker for the grave of your family member. Stones vary in price according to size, material, and the amount of engraving you choose. You can delay your decisions about a marker, but I encourage people to go ahead and decide as they face the difficulty of making arrangements because some have difficulty dealing with such decisions as they process through their grief in the weeks and months following the funeral.

Be prepared for the extreme expense you will face as you make funeral arrangements. Funerals cost thousands of dollars these days. Many funeral homes will work with you to make payments or allow you to wait until you receive a life insurance check. Most ministers do not charge a set fee for their services, and most funeral homes do not pay the minister for his services. Likely you will be asked if you want to provide an honorarium for the minister. Some people are offended at the thought of "paying the preacher." They feel it is the duty of the local pastor to provide this service as a part of his ministry to the community.

I think it is appropriate to pay the pastor something. You don't expect the mechanic to fix your car for free or the doctor to see you at no charge. If you are uncomfortable paying your local minister for his services, then perhaps you should consider using a friend or family member to oversee the funeral. If you want a professional to do the job, you should be willing to pay him for his service. Another expense you may incur is thank you cards. Most funeral homes offer thank you cards as a part of their available services. Sometimes there is an additional cost, and sometimes the cards are included in the package price. With today's rising costs, it is wise to consider purchasing insurance for your funeral or going ahead and prearranging your service through your local funeral chapel.

Guidelines for Conducting Funerals

One factor when a pastor officiates funeral services cannot be overlooked: you must spend time with the family members of the deceased. Even if you knew the individual very well, it is imperative to connect with those loved ones and listen to their stories. I like to take notes as the family shares. You may glean some good stories to share during the funeral service. The easy temptation is to simply go through the motions of a funeral service. This becomes increasingly appealing the longer you do them. Familiarity with a church member will also lead you to base your comments on your own experience and knowledge of the individual.

Meeting with the family may not afford you any new insight into the life of the one who passed on; however, time with the family does more than give you material for the funeral service. You need to connect with them in the context of their grief. They need to see you sitting in their living room or at their dining table. They need to tell you stories you've already heard before. Your eyes and your ears will likely do more to minister to the family than any words you might say. I strongly suggest that you take a pen and paper with you and write down what they tell you. It is unlikely that you will be able to use everything they tell you, but you need to be careful to record an accurate account of what they share with you.

I tremble when I hear what some ministers say during the course of funerals. I heard an older preacher say that a little ninety-something-year-old lady was now thirty-three years old in heaven because that's how old Jesus was when He died and rose again. Think about what that does to that family. The years of growing old gracefully and the wisdom of maturity are swept away by the whimsical imagination of someone who does not have one shred of credible evidence for such theology. Imagine the parents of a small boy hearing the pastor say their son is now thirty-three years old. They don't look forward to seeing a man they never knew; they want to see their little boy in heaven.

I've listened to well-meaning Christians try to comfort others who are struggling with grief. Unfortunately, some of those believers say some of the dumbest things I've ever heard. "God needed another rose in His garden, so He took your baby." Reflect on the theology of that statement for a moment. Put yourself in the position of that mother or father who is wrestling with the question of why. He or she might ask, "What kind of a sick God would kill my baby for some strange 'garden' in heaven?" More harm is done when the wrong things are said. If you don't know what to say, please take my advice and simply keep your mouth shut. A sincere hug and the fact you were there will do more for ministry than ten thousand words.

Another word of advice: review the obituary with the family before you step up to the microphone at the funeral. Some of the names of relatives (as well as some cities) can be difficult to pronounce. If there are abbreviations used to describe the deceased's accomplishments, ask what they stand for, and write them out in your notes. Sometimes there are abbreviations for military service with which you will not be familiar. The pulpit is not the place to try to figure them out.

You may have to intervene from time to time in the course of conducting funerals. For example, I had a gentleman who insisted that we add the song "Anchors Away" to the order of service because the dearly departed had served in the navy and so had this gentleman. The man suggesting the patriotic song was not related to the deceased in any way. He simply thought it was a good idea. After several attempts to explain to the man that I could not add the song, I called upon the funeral director to step in and be the bad guy. The man was agitated, but we did not sing the song either. This was an opportunity to protect the family from an unnecessary distraction and aggravation during their time of mourning.

I have had the privilege of working with some wonderful funeral directors. I have also worked with some who were horrible. A few years ago, there was a trend of local funeral homes selling out to large commercial companies. These large corporations ran the local funeral homes much like a restaurant chain: managers were relocated at will, quality was sacrificed in order increase the profit margin, and the blessing of local knowledge and relationship became a thing of the past. The few difficulties I have experienced have come through the funeral homes were connected to the large corporations.

For example, one day I entered the sanctuary of the church with another minister who was assisting me. As we came in, the family was already seated in the front pews. Typically when the minister is in position on the platform, the funeral director will enter from the rear of the room with the family of the deceased. The minister will then ask the congregation to stand in honor of the family. On this particular occasion, we entered five minutes before the service was to start and after the family had been seated. After the funeral was over, I asked the funeral director to tell me why he brought the family in before we came in the room. He said that the widow insisted on being escorted in early. He assured me that he tried to encourage her to wait for us to come in, but she pressed him to go ahead and seat the family.

The church provided a meal for the family following the committal service at the cemetery. I spoke to the widow, who was a member of my church. She was apologizing for the family being seated before the other minister and I made it in, and she then shared that she tried to talk the funeral director into waiting, but he insisted on hurrying along because of a tight schedule. Needless to say, I believed my church member. I had a few words with the funeral director later, but he never acknowledged responsibility for the situation. I was not very kind in what I had to say to the man. I did not appreciate the way he intimidated my church member, and I didn't appreciate him blaming her for his mistakes. I went back to my church member's home and told her of my conversation with the funeral director. She was thankful that I spoke up on her behalf to defend her integrity. In this case, I became an advocate for the grieving family.

It has been said that there is, "No such thing as a bad short sermon." There is truth in that statement because funerals sometimes become a production. Many families desire for one or more members to address the congregation. Some will read poems or share stories about their loved one. As I said before, there is a growing trend of families inviting anyone and everyone who so desires to step up and share testimonies about the deceased. Many funeral homes put together a video tribute by scanning photographs into a computer and making a slide show set to music. These video tributes can last for a few minutes or as long as half an hour. When you add up the time of testimonies, reading of the obituary, songs, videos, and the simple logistics of getting people seated and later dismissed at the end, you have accumulated a good bit of time. Did you notice that the funeral message was not included in this inventory? If the minister has prayed and prepared for his part of the service, he should be able to share a meaningful funeral sermon in ten minutes or less.

I like to ask the family if their loved one had a favorite passage of Scripture. Many will tell you that they do not know of a favorite verse, but some will know immediately. I also enjoy the blessing of looking through a person's Bible, because an active Christian who listened carefully and took good notes will have a wealth of material in his or her Bible. Some of my best funeral messages came as the result of reading what someone had written in the margins his or her Bible.

Be prepared for some oddities and quirks in some funerals. You may be surprised at the desires of some of your church members as you help them plan the service for their loved one. Music tends to be the most common area of unique and strange requests. I have heard the deceased's favorite college team's fight song played as a recessional for the funeral. Many will choose their favorite secular songs from the radio because it was important in the life of their loved one. You must develop a policy on what you will allow or will not allow in your church facilities and stick with it. I choose not to censor the music ahead of time. Some will think that I am horrible and irresponsible for this position; in my opinion, the musical selections cannot change who God is or the eternal destiny of the departed one. I jokingly tell my friends that I have done funerals with Elvis, Frank Sinatra, Louis Armstrong, Guns and Roses, Elton John, and a host of other famous singers (all by recording, of course).

You may encounter requests from the family with which you are uncomfortable. This is more common when dealing with people who do not attend your church but want you to do the funeral. The desire to please others can sometimes overshadow one's own convictions; however, I strongly suggest you stick to your spiritual convictions and do not be afraid to say no. For example, if a family asks you to read something inappropriate as a part of the funeral ceremony, you will have to make a choice. I have found that most people will accept your convictions, whether they agree with them or not. The fact that they are asking about your willingness shows there is a shadow of doubt in their minds. In other words, they probably already know that you would be uncomfortable with participating in something contrary to your beliefs. When it is all said and done, you have to live with the consequences of your choices; therefore, I choose to please God rather than man.

Early Encounters with Death

My first encounter with death came at age eleven. My maternal grandmother and I were close to one another. We called her Nannie. I was her youngest grandchild. Her husband had died when I was only eighteen months old, so I never knew my maternal grandfather. Nannie had moved to town, and she lived alone when I became old enough to go visit her. We would talk for hours. Her father was a Civil War veteran who rode with the cavalry of the Confederacy out of Texas. She told me stories of life on the farm before her father died. She was only six when he passed away. There were even stories of the infamous James and Younger gangs taking refuge at their house and swapping horses with my great-grandfather.

Nannie became ill during my fifth-grade year. I remember my dad coming to pick me up from school, which he never did. I can still see the look in his eyes as he told me to get in his pickup. I immediately felt that something was horribly wrong. Dad told me that Nannie had passed away, and I knew what that meant. The atmosphere at the house was somber, to say the least.

That evening when we went to the local funeral home to view the body, I had no idea what to expect. I had seen movies and television programs where soldiers had died or the bad guy had been shot by the good guy, but I had never seen an actual corpse. I remember my heart pounding as we parked the car and walked to the door. My other grandmother was with us. She could sense the fear in me. Grandma reassured me that it was going to be all right. I asked her what Nannie would look like. She told me that Nannie would simply look like she was taking a nap. I had seen my Nannie sleeping lots of times, so I found comfort in that thought. We entered the viewing room and walked up to the open casket. Nannie looked like she was sleeping, but she also looked different. I don't remember crying that night.

The funeral was held a day or two later in the funeral chapel. It was one of those older funeral homes where the family seating area was separate from the rest of the seats. I remember my heart hurting so much that I thought it would break. I cried so hard that my nose stopped up, and I could not see or breathe. I was exhausted afterward. That night seventeen tornadoes touched down in my hometown. We were awakened at 3:00 a.m. to the sound of a cyclone and hail beating against the house. We huddled in the hallway with a mattress over us. We had a perfectly good cellar, but the storm came so suddenly that there was no warning. The power was out at our house for six miserable days. It seemed fitting to our mood as a family. So much joy was absent with the passing of Nannie that the cold and darkness matched our feelings.

My paternal grandfather died when I was fourteen. I was never very close to him, though I loved him and he loved me. He lost most of one of his legs due to poor circulation, so I only knew him in a wheelchair. The one memory I carry from his death is my grandmother's statement when he passed away: "Well, Gus, now you've got two good legs to stand on."

I keep referring to my paternal grandmother. Her name was Alice. She was a feisty woman who loved the Lord with all her heart. Grandma was a fanatical baseball fan. Her living room was decorated with pennants of her favorite teams on the walls. If you went to visit her during a baseball game on television, your only hope for conversation came during the commercials. Grandma lived across the street from her church. She would see children playing basketball on the church parking lot, and she would go over to play with them. She didn't sit back and take granny shots like an old woman; Grandma would dribble, drive, and shoot jump shots. During the breaks in the games, she would tell those kids about Jesus. By the way, Grandma was in her seventies when she was doing this evangelistic outreach on the church parking lot. I remember her calling me with the names of people she was witnessing to and praying for their salvation. We would pray together and talk about soul winning during my teenage years. She had a beautiful, active faith in Christ.

Grandma went to visit one of my aunts in southeastern Oklahoma. My aunt and uncle lived in the mountains in a log cabin they built by hand. Rustic is not a strong enough term to describe their existence. Grandma loved it down there. I think it reminded her of simpler times. On this particular visit, my aunt got up early to fix breakfast and noticed that Grandma's light was on in the bedroom. My aunt thought it strange that Grandma would be awake so early. She went in to check on her mother and found my precious grandma dead, with her Bible laid across her chest. Grandma had been doing her nightly devotion when the Lord called her home. Can you imagine? To be reading about the glories of God one instant and then to be transported into His presence the next is possibly be the best death a Christian could hope for. Grandma never suffered with long-term illness or lost her independence in her later years. I think God honored a faithful woman with a blessed passing.

When Grandma died, I was on a ski trip in Colorado with my church group. One of my cousins was there as well. We got the message that Grandma, or Ma, as we called her, had passed away, so a travel agent in our home church began to make arrangements for us to fly home for the funeral. This was in the spring of 1983, one of the worst times of foul weather in Colorado's history. The airport in Denver was basically shut down for days. We flew in on a small plane and had to circle the airport for forty-five minutes in order to land. We missed our flight and had to try to catch another plane. We got the runaround from several ticket agents. When I finally prayed and asked God for wisdom and direction, I felt led to go down a certain corridor of the airport (this was before all the security we endure today). I saw a woman standing under a sign that said, "Oklahoma City" on it. The light fell on her in an unusually powerful way. God impressed on my heart that she was the answer to my prayer. I explained our situation to her, and we were allowed to board that plane to fly home for Grandma's funeral.

Mom's Story

On Thanksgiving in 1994, my family and I went home to my parents' house, as we often did for the holiday. My mother was a great cook. She grew up in the country with a mom who was a wonderful cook. They didn't measure the ingredients, and most of the family recipes were not written down on paper. On this particular occasion, my mother's house was filled with the wonderful sounds and smells of her orchestrating another masterpiece for dinner. As I watched mom shuffling around the kitchen, I noticed her limping slightly. When I commented that she seemed gimpy and asked if she had pulled a muscle, Mom got very serious. She told me she had been struggling with pain in the area of her hip and groin for some time, but the doctor had not figured out the cause yet. She told me that Dad had been insisting they take her to a clinic like Scott White in Texas for a complete examination. Mom was hesitant.

My mother's pain and discomfort increased over the next few weeks. She and her physician determined that exploratory surgery was necessary to identify the problem because noninvasive tests produced no solid conclusions. In December, a surgeon performed an exploratory operation on my mom. He came out from the operating room to tell me and my dad that he had hoped to find a mass but did not. His exact words were that the area looked "yucky." He took a tissue sample and sent it to Oklahoma City for examination. After several stressful days of waiting, the diagnosis came back: lymphoma. We learned more about that disease than we cared to. I read about it in an attempt to understand some of the challenges facing my mother. I began to realize that cancer in the lymph system meant it was ambulatory and spreading by the minute—and it did.

Mom was transferred to Mercy Hospital in Oklahoma City because their oncology ward is considered top notch in our state. The doctors and nurses were wonderful, considerate, kind, and careful to explain every part of the journey ahead. My mom took her first chemotherapy treatment in January of 1995. The medication lowered her white blood cell count to a value of less than one. The doctor said she could not endure another treatment or it would kill her. He suggested radiation but cautioned us that taking pinpoint aim at a mobile disease would not be very effective. He was right. Mom endured about half of the prescribed radiation treatments before the doctor did an evaluation and determined that it was doing no good whatsoever.

In the meantime, the cancer spread throughout her body. It was in her bone marrow, brain, heart, liver, and lungs, and it had damaged her spinal column, causing her to completely lose the use of her lower body. All of this happened within two months. I watched my mom deteriorate in every way imaginable. Her body went downhill quickly, as did her hope and will to live. I also saw my father age rapidly during these difficult weeks. He would sit by his wife's bed and watch her suffer. There were pain and fatigue in his face that I cannot describe with words.

During those weeks between the first chemo treatment and her death, there were a few moments where we shared special times together in spite of the hurt. One day when my father left the hospital room to go for a walk and take a break, I sat with Mom. She told me to take her makeup bag and look in the bottom of it under the makeup. I found a piece of yellow notebook paper with her handwriting on it. Mom informed me that my dad couldn't handle the inevitable, so she was counting on me to take responsibility for her funeral.

Mom knew that I had done many funerals and helped many families make arrangements during times of grief and heartache. The paper outlined her wishes for her funeral service. She had written the name of the minister she wanted to officiate (she knew I couldn't get through it as her son), the songs she wanted, and even the names of the pallbearers. I put the paper in my billfold and kept it a secret from Dad. Mom also told me she had purchased a whole life insurance policy that was paid for and should be enough to pay for the expenses. The policy was in the safety deposit box at their bank back home.

On the Thursday before she died, I had the opportunity to have my mom to myself for a few minutes in her hospital room. My mother was a frightened person throughout her lifetime. She was the kind who nearly panicked when the storm clouds came in the spring. We always went to the cellar, just to be safe. She also never liked to stay alone in the house. Fear was one of her greatest enemies in life. I asked her if she was afraid. She said, "Of dying?" I said yes. My mother laughed and said, "No. Can you believe it?" I saw a peace that passes understanding in my mother's face and voice. The Lord truly blessed her with His presence and calm assurance in the last days of her life.

At one point, when I was not at the hospital, my mother stopped breathing. She had a living will and did not want to be resuscitated. My dad was by her side. He thought it was over, but after a short time, Mom drew a deep breath and opened her eyes. She told my dad that she had seen Jesus. She exclaimed that He had new legs for her in heaven, and she would walk again. It was one of the most spiritually meaningful moments in their lives.

It was a Saturday morning in March 1995 when my father called me to come to the hospital because Mom was dying. I had to officiate a wedding that afternoon and could not come until after the ceremony. Fortunately, I was living in the area, and the drive to the hospital was only twenty-five minutes. When I arrived, my mother was receiving a straight morphine drip through her IV. The medication helped with the pain but caused her great difficulty in her speech and thinking processes. She could not call our names, but she looked at my brother and me and said, "Boys." Several family members were in and out throughout the day. Mom was unconscious through Saturday into Sunday.

My brother and I did not sleep at all that Saturday night, and Dad was only able to rest a short time. Sunday was a difficult day because Mom contracted pneumonia and her lungs began to fill with fluid. Her breathing became more and more labored as the day wore on. At 6:20 p.m. on March 12, 1995, we stepped out of the room to allow the nurse to check on Mom. While we were in the hallway, she died. My brother had already left because he had to get back to his job and had a long drive ahead of him, but two couples from Mom and Dad's Sunday school class had come to visit and were there when she died. We gathered around her body, held hands, and prayed together. My dad voiced a sweet prayer of thanksgiving to the Lord for healing her eternally and for the fact that she was not suffering any more.

Dad and I went to the funeral home to make the arrangements for Mom's celebration service. My father had the most lost look in his eyes as we sat across from the funeral director. It was then I produced the piece of paper Mom had given me while Dad was out of the hospital room. My dad commented that it was just like her to take care of everything, even her own funeral arrangements. That little slip of yellow notebook paper was more precious to us than anything on earth during those difficult moments. It gave us confidence that we were honoring her wishes.

At the time of my mother's death, the church she and Dad attended was undergoing an extensive remodeling project, so the sanctuary was completely torn apart. We decided to have the service at the funeral chapel. We feared it would not be large enough, and we were right.

To perfectly honest, I was somewhat numb at Mom's funeral. I was still trying to absorb the fact that she was dead. I remember feeling as if every eye in the place was transfixed on my family and me. I did not feel as if people were looking at us in any negative way but rather in sympathy and concern. It was quite a change for me personally. Normally I sit on the stage and watch everyone coming into the funeral service. This time we sat together at the front of the chapel on the front row with our backs to the crowd. I don't remember the songs, and I cannot tell you what the minister said during his message.

My most memorable moment came when they opened the casket and the people began to file by and speak to us as the family. A stream of church members from my congregation, some who drove from ninety-plus miles away, began to file by to console me. I ultimately stood up because they were having a hard time hugging me while I was sitting down. I later found they brought the church bus filled with church members who wanted to support me in my time of grief. As a pastor, I had never felt so loved by a congregation.

God taught me so much through the process of my mom's death. I discovered, as I sat by her bed watching her die, that so much of what I deemed important turned out to be trivial by comparison. I used to get worked up over so many things, but staring life and death in the face can have a calming effect by putting life into a proper perspective. I became a better pastor after mom died. I visited hospitals with a deeper sense of purpose. I prayed more intensely for those with cancer.

I learned that it is all right to stand and weep in a hospital room with a frightened family. I found that crying at the funeral home with people is good medicine for them and me.

I learned a great deal by sitting in front of the pulpit rather than standing behind it. When people are hurting, they won't likely remember what we say in our sermons, and the songs may only be a distant memory when the funeral is over. Grieving families are often numb during the funeral service. God uses the hugs of friends to help heal broken hearts. People won't remember what you said, but they will remember that you were there.

There is comfort in connecting with someone who has walked a similar path. Those passages describing Jesus as one who knows our pain and sorrows provide great reassurance to the Christian. My approach to funerals changed after going through my mother's death. My heart continues to be touched deeply as I look into the eyes of hurting people at funerals.

Reaching Out through Funerals

I have long believed that funerals provide good opportunity to minister to the unchurched in the community. There are challenges in preaching funerals for strangers; however, there are also good opportunities to reach out with God's love.

I received a phone call one evening from a church member who worked as the telephone operator at the local hospital. She told me of a family whose fourteen-year-old son was dying of Huntington's disease. The family had no church affiliation but wanted a preacher to come pray for them. I gladly agreed.

I introduced myself to the family in their son's hospital room. I knew their son's name sounded familiar to me. I finally realized that my youngest daughter had helped their son in the special needs class at her school. My daughter was a peer tutor and had often pushed this young man's wheelchair for him around the school. When the boy's mother knew it was my daughter, she thanked me over and over for the way my daughter had helped her son. I was a proud dad that night. I prayed for the family and promised to keep them in my prayers. Their son died a short time later, and they asked me to officiate the funeral. On the Sunday after his memorial service, I saw his mom in our worship service. She shared with me that she wanted to go to heaven to see her boy again. There are golden opportunities to reach people through funerals for strangers.

Sometimes the willingness to officiate at funerals for strangers can lead you into awkward circumstances. Several years ago, I was asked to come to one of the local funeral homes to meet with a widow to discuss her husband's service. They had no church affiliation but wanted a Baptist preacher to speak at his funeral. When I arrived at the funeral home, the widow was back viewing her husband's body. They had just gotten him prepared, and she was seeing her husband's corpse for the first time. She came into the meeting room, wiping the tears from her eyes. She thanked the funeral director for "doing such a good job" on her husband. She commented that it seemed he had a smile on his face in the casket. She then proceeded to share her belief about why he had a smile: she just knew her husband was up in heaven having a beer with John Wayne. By the grace of God, I kept a straight face. I only went through four years of college and six years of graduate school, so I guess I missed the class about heaven being comprised of cold beer and a Western hero.

Location of the Dead in Christ

I probably field more questions about the afterlife than I do about death itself. Most people want to know where their loved ones are and what they are doing. Many want reassurance that there will be a reunion with those who have gone before them. I must establish one truth as clearly as possible: only those who have had a personal, faith relationship with Jesus Christ will live forever. The world wants to believe that all people, regardless of religious preference, ultimately end up in heaven. Nothing could be further from the truth. Only those who have accepted Jesus as the only source of salvation can be saved. He said that there was only one way to God the Father, and that is through Jesus the Son. With that understanding in place, the truths of this chapter address the biblical evidence of life in the eternal presence of God.

Where Is My Loved One Right Now?

People need reassurance about the well being of their loved ones who have died in Christ. There is ample evidence to give us confidence that relatives who die go immediately to be with the Lord. For example, Jesus's story about the rich man and Lazarus (Luke 16:19–31) portrays Lazarus as a man of faith. The Bible says that when Lazarus died, the "angels carried him to Abraham's side."

In Luke's account of the crucifixion, there are two statements from Jesus that further establish the idea of immediate transport into the presence of God. To the thief dying on another cross next to Him, Jesus said, "I tell you the truth, today you will be with me in paradise" (Luke 23:43). Luke also records the words Jesus spoke as He died for our sins: "Father, into your hands I commit my spirit" (Luke 23:46).

Some will argue that the placement of the punctuation in the reference about being in paradise completely changes the meaning of the passage. In other words, Jesus was simply saying on that particular day that someday He and the thief would be together in paradise. I personally believe that Jesus meant on that very day they would be together in the presence of God in heaven. Some have tried to argue that Jesus went to abode of the dead or even to hell itself for three days before His resurrection. I find it difficult to believe that the Son of God would describe hell as going into His Father's hands. Jesus went to heaven for three days until He came back to earth in His resurrected form.

Paul's letters to the Corinthians provide some of the strongest evidence for belief in the immediate transportation of a Christian's soul into the presence of God. In his first letter to the Corinthians, Paul goes into great detail concerning the resurrection of Jesus and the resurrection of believers. He describes the fact that the human body is not equipped to live eternally. The apostle uses the analogy of planting and harvesting to communicate the spiritual reality of man's resurrection at the return of Christ. The human body is "sown a natural body." It is "raised a spiritual body" (1 Cor. 15:44). The human body is "perishable" and "mortal" in this life. It will be "imperishable" and "immortal" in eternity (1 Cor. 15:50–57).

If the body of a loved one is destined to rest in the ground until the return of Christ, what happens to the soul of a believer who dies? Paul gives a powerful description in 2 Corinthians 5:1–10. He uses the language of being "away from the body and at home with the Lord" (2 Cor. 5:8). What does the apostle mean by this? I believe Scripture is teaching that the soul of a believer goes immediately to be with Jesus at the moment of death. The body stays here on earth and is placed in the ground, cremated, or buried at sea. At the time of the second coming of Christ, all the bodies of Christians will be raised with the same resurrection power Jesus experienced. At that time, there will be a reunion of body and soul. In the meantime, the souls of our dear loved ones are at home with the Lord.

Will I Recognize My Loved Ones?

Another popular question concerns our ability to recognize one another in heaven. Will we know our parents and grandparents? Will they know us? The answer is an emphatic *yes*.

When Jesus, Peter, James, and John went together up a high mountain, they experienced a powerful moment in Christ's ministry as He was transfigured before their very eyes. The Bible records that Moses and Elijah also appeared on the mountain and talked with Jesus. How did the disciples know the men who appeared were Moses and Elijah? They recognized them. There is no record of the disciples asking Jesus who these two men were (Mark 9:2–13).

Though she did not recognize Him at first, Mary Magdalene was able to recognize Jesus after His resurrection (John 20:10–18). He called her name, and she grabbed Him in a loving expression of worship and adoration.

Jesus also appeared to His disciples following the resurrection. He is apparently able to enter through locked doors in His resurrected state (John 20:19). John's account describes Jesus showing His followers the scars from the crucifixion. It is fair to say that though the resurrection body is immortal and imperishable, it will not be free from the scars of this life.

We can surmise from these passages that we will indeed be able to recognize our loved ones in heaven, and they will be able to recognize us. There are several other verses to support this truth. It is important to remember that life in eternity will be vastly different from our experiences here below. For example, Jesus said there will be neither marriage nor giving in marriage in heaven (Luke 20:35). It is a mistake to believe you will be reunited with your wife or your husband in a marriage relationship like the one you have enjoyed here on earth. Life in heaven will be for worshiping and glorifying God, not tending to our own desires and wishes. There will be no sense of loss or grief in heaven because we are promised that all tears will be wiped away by God Himself (Rev. 21:4). You will not be upset or disappointed in heaven because you cannot be married to your spouse any longer. The old things (life on earth) will pass away, and everything in our experience will be brand new.

What about the Second Coming?

Another important truth to establish is found in Paul's first letter to the Thessalonians. The apostle addressed the fear of the believers there concerning the question of the involvement of the dead in Christ in the second coming. The Thessalonians were apparently concerned that their loved ones who had already died would in some way be less fortunate than the living believers at the time of the return of the Lord. Paul reassures the saints that the dead in Christ (along with the living Christians at that time) will have an equal part in the second coming.

First Thessalonians 4:13–18, a familiar passage, is often read at funerals and graveside services. Most Christians have heard this passage on numerous occasions throughout their lifetimes. One interesting aspect of the Word is found in verse 14 as Paul tells us, "God will bring with Jesus those who have fallen asleep in Him." The picture is that of

Jesus coming in the air to call His church home. With Him will be all the believers who have died prior to His return to earth. The eastern sky will not only be filled with the glory of the Lord, but also with countless souls of our loved ones who have already gone home to be with Jesus. God's children will participate in the second coming by either coming with Jesus from heaven to earth or rising up from the earth to meet the Lord and our loved ones in the air.

Difficult Funerals

You may encounter ministry opportunities with families suffering from the stigma of an "unacceptable" death. When a loved one commits suicide, is murdered, or dies of AIDS or a drug overdose, the grieving family is often left with the compounded pain of the judgment of others around them. One truth I cannot emphasize enough is the fact that we who minister to people don't always have the answers to their hard questions. I cannot explain the reality of why a son who was raised in church later chooses to indulge in drugs and ultimately dies as a result of his rebellion. I don't know why some precious young ladies come to the point of such deep despair that they take their own lives in suicide. It is incredibly unfair when an innocent person is brutally murdered at the hand of an uncaring criminal. Families in such situations often struggle in deeper ways than families whose loved ones die of natural causes.

I find that visualizations help me articulate reality more clearly in my own mind. For example, some movies do a great job of portraying the depth of pain in a grief-stricken life. I have a favorite old movie that I watch every year in preparation for hunting season. Robert Redford starred in *Jeremiah Johnson* in 1972. It is the story of a man fed up with his world who decides to move to the mountains of Colorado to be a mountain man. Part of the story line involves Jeremiah's character encountering an Indian tribe. The chief gives Jeremiah a gift of his own daughter for marriage. Jeremiah also inherits a young boy whose mother became insane after her husband and two other children were murdered by Indians.

Jeremiah's little family quickly becomes close to one another as they carve out a living in the mountain wilderness of nineteenth-century Colorado. Johnson helps a cavalry unit find its way across the mountain passes to rescue a stranded wagon train. Upon his return home, Jeremiah finds his wife and adopted son brutally murdered by the Crow Indians. There is a scene in which Robert Redford's character sits in his log cabin simply staring into space as his wife and son lay dead on the floor. There is no dialogue or flashback to happier times. The director simply filmed the actor from several angles as he sat in shock and disbelief. Go watch that movie, but pay close attention to Redford's masterful portrayal of grief. You may find that people in your ministry circle will experience similar circumstances. Do not be afraid of awkward silence. Don't think that you must say something to "fix" the situation.

While you cannot answer the hard questions, you can be the presence of Christ in the lives of those who are hurting around you. As a minister, you must resist the temptation to join in with others who would criticize or sit in judgment of a family suffering grief from an "unacceptable" death. You may find the families are unwilling to talk to you or open up about their feelings. Recognize that they may not know what they are feeling at the moment. Your presence there will be enough. The fact that you were willing to go to them in spite of the painful circumstances of the death of their loved one communicates your compassion. It is likely that your ministry will be needed later, long after the flowers from the funeral service have faded and died. Stay sensitive to the possibility of referring your church members to a professional Christian counselor.

The likelihood of ministering to a grieving family divided by a divorce increases more and more as the divorce rate continues to climb. It is a sad commentary, but statistics show that the divorce rate among Christians runs a close parallel to those with no professed church association. I have personally watched families become angry with one another during the various stages of the funeral process. It is incredibly awkward when one person is screaming profanity at another member of the family.

Anger is heightened by the grief. The pain and disappointment of the divorce often find an outlet in the context of the funeral for a member of the divided family. Do not be surprised if the funeral director has to reserve two separate sections in the church for the family members. I have even officiated a service where the funeral home provided two separate sets of chairs at the graveside so the two factions would not have to sit together. Do not allow yourself to be drawn into the fight of a broken family. Your job is to provide as much spiritual comfort as possible. You cannot fix their longstanding problems with one funeral service.

One of the most difficult funerals I have performed was actually my very first funeral as a pastor while I was still in seminary. It involved the death of an infant. The child did not die of SIDS or from a genetic disorder; he died because he starved to death in his own home. The mother did her best to keep her baby alive, but the young husband loved to drink and "have a good time." He would not allow his wife to have enough money to buy groceries for the baby. She would take whatever she could find and run it through a blender, but it was not enough.

The husband was drunk every night with his friends. The money that should have been buying formula and baby food went for beer. I went to the home of this young couple with a copy of *Tracks of a Fellow Struggler*, an excellent work on the grief of losing a child in death. The young man quickly informed me that he did not want my book. I will confess that I was angry on that porch. In my flesh, I wanted to knock that guy's block off. I was only twenty five at the time and not much older than that drunken, irresponsible father.

The family wanted a graveside service only. I had to pray harder than ever as I watched the young man crying and carrying on in front of the extended family and guests. I wanted to scream out that it was largely his fault. God quickly convicted me of my humanness. That young couple was not a part of my church and they needed to be reached. I tried desperately but was never able to get them to come to church. The Lord convicted me to stop judging them and start praying for them.

I have a dear friend in the ministry who does more funerals than any pastor I know. He shared with me that he performed the service for a murder victim. If that was not difficult enough, it was fairly obvious to everyone involved that the murderer was a member of the family. He was never brought to justice because it could not be proven beyond a shadow of a doubt. That man sat with the rest of the family as my friend did the funeral service. My friend said the tension was almost unbearable. Can you imagine?

In the case of the baby's funeral, I used the passage from 2 Samuel 12:15b–23. It is the story of David's baby who died and David's reaction to the death. The key phrase in the passage is, "I will go to him, but he will not return to me" (2 Sam. 12:23b). God's Word makes it clear that David fully expected to see his son again in heaven. I have used this passage many times in funeral services for babies. It provides strong evidence that little ones are innocent in the Lord until they come to a point of being able to understand sin and its consequences.

Suicide carries a horrible stigma for the members of the family left behind. In high school, a classmate of mine wrecked the family car. Out of fear of his father, the young man went home to his garage and took his own life with a shotgun. That was my first encounter with suicide. There is an old myth that suicide will cause a person to go straight to hell. This is not true. There can always be a debate on the person's salvation. Was the individual who took his/her own life truly born again? Ultimately only God can answer that question.

It is my opinion that a truly born-again Christian can commit suicide. It is a horrible mistake because it is a sin against God. However, it is powerless to separate an individual from the love of God. Romans 8:38–39 is a powerful reminder of the durability of God's love for us as His children. No sin is able to drive God's love away from us or us from God's love. A pastor friend of mine had a young person in his church commit suicide, and my friend was called upon to preach the funeral message. He comforted those in attendance by saying that the teenager had made a horrible mistake. The pastor reminded the congregation that all of us are guilty of making horrible mistakes. Our mistakes simply take different forms.

I once attended a funeral that was the result of one of the most unthinkable situations imaginable. An old college buddy of mine was going through a divorce and never got over it. He had his kids with him for the weekend and made a tragic decision. My friend took a gun and killed his own children before turning the weapon on himself. All of us who knew the man were shaken to the core. The pastor of the church where my friend attended did a masterful job of reminding us of all the good things the man had done in his lifetime. I believe my friend is in heaven today because I knew his testimony very well from our friendship in college. He made the worst decision a father could make.

You may find yourself involved in funerals like the ones I have described. You will likely be involved in situations equally or more challenging than these. Stay focused on your task. Resist the temptation to be the one who fixes the situation. Avoid being drawn in by family members who want you to take their side. Your job is to be the voice of God by sticking to the Word. You can listen to people and allow them to vent their deep feelings without joining them in their position. Be kind, patient, caring, and compassionate. Some may desire your approval or your agreement, but what they really need is for you to remain strong in the faith. Don't be afraid to tackle hard funerals. God will get you through it. If He uses you to reach one person with the gospel, it will be worth it all.

Long ago I came to the spiritual conclusion that nothing I say or do at a funeral service can change the eternal destiny of the deceased. That person's eternity was settled in his lifetime. If he accepted Jesus as his personal Lord and Savior, then he will go to heaven forever. If a person has rejected the invitation to accept Jesus, he will spend eternity separated from God in a place called hell. The preacher's comments during the funeral cannot change that. Avoid the temptation to say more than you should when you are unsure of a person's eternal destiny. Pastors often have a tendency to attempt to preach the departed person into heaven for the comfort of the family. This is unwise. It is equally inappropriate to paint a picture of the deceased as burning in hell. Sometimes you may read the person's name as you share the obituary and never refer to him or her again throughout the course of your comments.

There seems to be a correlation between the difficulty of the death and the intensity of emotion displayed by the family. This is not always true. However, it has been my observation that the greater the shock, the greater the outbursts. I would also argue that people without Christ tend to grieve more painfully than people with a saving relationship with Jesus. Be prepared for intense emotionality, especially from those not connected to your church.

You will likely find that moments standing next to the open casket are the most difficult to bear. It is almost a guarantee that you will see at least one "toucher" in the crowd who feels the insatiable need to touch the dead person's body in the casket. Some will kiss the deceased, while others will pat the person's shoulder or face. Occasionally you will witness a hugger who looks like she is trying to crawl into the casket herself (I've never seen a man do this). At times the most challenging part of your assignment will be resisting the temptation to smile or laugh out loud. You will experience heart-wrenching moments as well. You will be moved when a wife tells her husband good-bye or a mother kisses the cold body of her baby. The uncontrolled sobs of a grieving spouse can pierce your soul. You will likely overhear some of the most incredible words of love from the lips of those who lean over the bodies of their loved ones.

Balance is necessary for the minister at a funeral service. If you become too emotionally involved, you will be unable to perform your duties. If you stay too detached, you will come across as cold and uncaring. You must pray and ask God to give you wisdom to properly connect to those in need. Remember that it is Christ who works in you and through you to minister to people.

The Candid Camera Funeral

Before I begin to tell this story, I will confess that words will not do it justice. You had to be there; however, you should be thankful that you weren't. I've conducted hundreds of funerals. Thank God that I have only experienced one like this one.

We had three young children who began attending our church. Our bus would pick up the three kids every week. They were not far apart in age. Each of them had a different last name but the same mother. At that time, there was another man living with their mom who was not married to her. We would go and invite the mother and boyfriend to come to church. Most of the time they were too drunk to understand us or too high to care that we had come to invite them to join us.

I received a phone call one morning informing me that the mother had been killed in a one-car accident north of our city. It seems that she and another lady had been out all night drinking at a club north of town. In the wee hours of the morning, they attempted to navigate the short drive home. The driver lost control of the vehicle and ran off a bridge. The passenger, who was the mother of the three children attending our church, was killed. The driver fled the scene on foot for fear of being arrested for drunken driving. The police found her in an apartment badly bruised and suffering from a broken leg. The local authorities asked me to go tell the children that their mother had been killed in the accident. I've had to do this several times, and I hate it.

The children received the news better than I feared. Our church did a great job of rallying around those kids. I think every mom in the church was ready to adopt them. The time came to arrange the funeral service. It was to be held in a funeral home in a metropolitan community a few miles away. The funeral director shared with me that his funeral home was going to provide the services pro bono. The time and date were set.

I arrived at the funeral home nearly an hour before the service was scheduled to start. Several members of our congregation made the thirty-minute drive to show support for the children. Family members began to trickle into the chapel. The funeral director and I discussed the order of service. I would be the lone speaker of the day, and there would be several songs, all on tape. The musical selections included "November Rain" by Guns and Roses, "Tiny Dancer" by Elton John, "Brown-Eyed Girl" by Van Morrison, a country song by John Anderson that talked about taking off a woman's dress and making love to her, and "Amazing Grace."

I'll get back to the musical fiasco in a minute. The deceased had a brother who wanted to say something at his sister's service. He was in a maximum-security prison in Oklahoma, but the authorities made an exception to allow this man out on the streets. His arrival included several armed guards. He was in a jumpsuit with leg irons, a chain around his waist, and handcuffs. He jingled when he walked. At the appointed time, he took the pulpit in the funeral chapel. I was sitting on the stage behind him. He was prisoner number 0613. He said he had written a poem for his sister. He proceeded to read an old poem that had been published countless times in "Dear Abbey" and other places. Even so, he took full credit for its creation. I had to resist the temptation to thank him for his speech and ask if number 0614 would like to say anything. Don't think me crass; I needed humor before this funeral was over.

Back to the musical selections. I later called them "dedication hour," because a member of the family stood up before each song and said a few words about the importance or significance of each selection. The Guns and Roses song was the oldest son's request. He was a young teenager who liked hard rock music. The old Van Morrison song, "Brown-Eyed Girl," was a natural choice because the lady had brown eyes. You may not know the lyrics of this song, but there is a line that talks about "making love in the green grass behind the stadium." Hearing those words in a car driving down the road would not foster much response, but I became increasingly uncomfortable as they blared over the funeral home chapel's speakers.

It came time for Elton John's "Tiny Dancer." The guy running the sound system at the back of the chapel put the tape in on the wrong side. Instead of "Tiny Dancer," we were blessed with "Pinball Wizard." The sound man never paid attention to what was playing, so I had to leave the platform, walk to the back of the chapel, and tell him of his mistake. There was never a longer walk on the face of the earth than my trip to the back of that chapel. The John Anderson country selection included some disturbing lyrics about taking off his girlfriend's green dress and making love to her. It was incredibly awkward and inappropriate. The musical conundrum rounded off with good old "Amazing Grace." I was never so glad to hear the old standard as I was that day.

The time finally came for me to preach the message. I had shared the obituary earlier between musical dedications. I focused the message toward those three children. I encouraged them to stay close to each other and close to Jesus. We already knew they would be moving to an aunt's home in Texas. My heart went out to them. As I said my last "amen," another family member bolted up on stage. She informed me that the boyfriend of the dearly departed had written a song. She shared that he had his guitar in his pickup, and it would just take a minute to fetch it and sing his song.

I looked at the funeral director to bail me out. I hoped he would suggest that we move on to the viewing of the body because the service had run well over an hour by this point in time. The funeral director was no help at all. The boyfriend was encouraged to go get his guitar while the rest of us waited. He came back and sat down on the steps of the platform at the front of the chapel. I remember thinking, *This ought to be good.* I cannot describe the song for you. Imagine a metal rock band kind of rhythm played on an acoustic guitar. There was no rhyme or reason to the melody. The words were nonsensical. I remember something about him and the girl riding the tail of a comet through stars. I have always respected the sanctity of the funeral event, but I was ready to laugh and cry all at the same time.

When the boyfriend finished his ode to his woman, the funeral director came up and opened the casket. I took my usual position by the head of the body. Normally people are dismissed row by row and file by the casket in an orderly fashion. Not this bunch. When that lid went up on the coffin, the crowd poured—en masse—to the front of the room to crowd around the body of the woman and me. They looked like people at a carnival trying to see a sideshow. People pushed and shoved each other and tried to get in the front of the crowd for a closer look.

At one point, a rather large woman felt the need to kiss the body of the deceased. As she struggled to hoist herself into position to plant a smooch on the forehead of the girl in the coffin, the lid hinge gave way, and the lid began to fall on top of the short, fat woman kissing the corpse. I reached out my left arm and caught the lid on the back of my wrist, just above my watch. I tried to fix the hinge so the lid would stay open on its own but had no success. The funeral director finally rescued me and fixed the problem.

The woman we buried that day was thirty-two years old. They buried her in a pair of blue jeans and a chambray shirt, and there was a high school homecoming mum pinned to her shirt. I figured that her high school days of going to the prom were probably the last good days she had in her troubled life. I left that day not believing all I had seen and experienced. I glanced around to see if there was a candid camera because it was all too strange to be true. There were no cameras.

To this day, when I hear "Brown-Eyed Girl" on the radio, I flash back to that funeral service. I'm not sure I could handle two of these services in one lifetime.

African Funeral

I have always associated mission work with the continent of Africa. I suppose this comes from learning about missionaries in Africa as a young boy growing up in church. God afforded me a unique experience on mission trip to Kenya a few years ago.

There were sixteen of us from our church. The organizer added two others from another community to the roster. Over the span of two weeks, our team of eighteen short-term missionaries was blessed to record over 12,700 professions of faith. I have never seen anything like it in my life. Every dirt trail we walked led to a village filled with people who had never heard of Jesus. I do not remember a single place where the people were not willing to listen to the gospel. The sheer numbers were enough to make this a trip of a lifetime, but God took me on a journey even deeper into the mysteries of His will.

I was assigned to a local pastor who served two congregations. David is a simple family man with a deep passion for the things of God. He walks everywhere because he does not have another means of transportation. He works countless hours teaching, preaching, and ministering to the flock of believers under his care. David is fluent in English and quite capable as a translator.

During my time with David doing our evangelistic work, he informed me that there had been a death in one of the villages nearby.

This death was even more emotionally charged because it was a twelve-year-old girl. Some of the members of that family group attended his church. He went to comfort the family in their time of grief.

In Kenyan culture, it is customary for the minister to "sit up" with the family through the first night following the death of the loved one. David stayed with the grieving family until 4:00 a.m., walked home to take a bath and change clothes, and met me at 9:00 a.m. to spend the day going from house to house sharing the gospel. When I asked him if he was tired, he explained to me that it was his duty to minister to the hurting family in this way. I marveled at his devotion and untiring sense of duty to his church. David also shared with me the plans for the funeral of the girl. He explained that the church was expected to provide a sound system, pall bearers, and music for the service. The actual funeral would take place in the yard of the houses of that family's village. Following the ceremony, the girl would be buried on the family property next to their house. He told me that the funeral would be the next day at 2:00 in the afternoon.

David and I met the next morning, as usual, to go around the villages to share the gospel. It was during this time that he explained to me that I was to preach the funeral message of the twelve-year-old girl that afternoon. I immediately began to decline the invitation and shared my fears of not knowing what to say or how to say it in his culture. David told me he had already offered my services to the family, and they were excited to know that a white missionary from the United States would be honoring their little girl.

When it became clear that there was no way out of this for me, I started asking countless questions about etiquette and protocol in an African funeral. The pastor was patient to answer all my questions and warn me of things to avoid while preaching the funeral message. Needless to say, I have never been more nervous about a funeral in my life.

When it came time for the service, we made our way to that particular village in plenty of time. As our driver pulled into the area, we were met by a large number of people gathered around the homes. The crowd grew larger and larger as the time for the service approached. I saw the "sound system" the church provided. It consisted of an old boom box you would see in a junk store and a car battery wired to it for a power source. Music was blaring from it prior to the start of the service.

Those of us involved were briefed on the order of the funeral. As I waited anxiously for my time to step to the microphone, I absorbed a thousand and one sights, sounds, and impressions that I could never adequately describe in words. My heart raced as I experienced professional mourners for the first time. Women with brightly colored clothes shook and wailed loudly outside the door of the family's home. Some men talked and smoked as if they were simply at the local store or gathering place. Children ran around chasing one another, seemingly unaware of the intensity of the human drama unfolding all around them. There were over a thousand people gathered in this tiny space for this girl's funeral. Her classmates from the local school were dismissed from class so they could attend.

The time for the funeral service came. The girl's body was in her family's house. The women of the village had washed the body and dressed it in new garments. Some young men from the church carried the coffin, a simple wooden box, out of the house and into the yard where the people gathered. A young man from the church read what sounded like an obituary. I don't understand Swahili, but I did recognize the use of proper names in the reading. There were several songs shared by various members of the congregation through the rented sound system.

My time to speak finally came. I stepped up to the microphone with intense prayer and a sense of utter dependence upon God. What had the pastor told me? Would I speak inappropriately and offend the family? Did he tell me it was rude to mention the girl's name? I paused for what seemed like an eternity and opened my mouth to speak. I cannot tell all that I said that day. I shared the Word of God. I told of my mother's death and my pain through that experience. I said that no parent should ever have to bury a child. I told them of Jesus and the empty tomb and the promise of eternal life through faith in Him. I expressed my sincere sense of hurt for the pain they were enduring in this moment. I encouraged families to love and appreciate each other because we never know when God will call us home. Apparently I did not say anything offensive during my part of the service. Thank God. I had a genuine feeling of relief when I sat down.

There were others who spoke that day but none for as long as me. The time for the burial came. Once again I experienced something like I never had before. The young men of the church opened the lid of the coffin to reveal the girl's body. She was so young. The guests and family members filed by to view the body, much like we typically do in our country. Once the viewing was over and the coffin was closed again, the pall bearers picked it up to carry it to the grave. I was instructed to join in the processional. The distance from the funeral service to the freshly dug grave couldn't have been more than thirty or forty feet, but the manner in which the coffin was moved made it seemed much farther.

All of us involved with the service filed in right behind the coffin. The family followed us, and then the rest of the people. Remember, there were over a thousand people there. The pall bearers began to chant as they carried the casket on their shoulders. The people quickly joined in the song. We were taking tiny steps. I'm not sure if the little steps were tradition or simply necessary because the crowd was so large and the space so small. The closest image I had seen in the United States was a movie portraying an old jazz funeral in New Orleans where the mourners played instruments and danced as the processional moved down the street.

The closer we came to the open grave, the tighter the crowd pressed round the coffin. We finally reached the burial plot, and the pall bearers set the box down on sticks to suspend it over the hole. Another man had been asked to speak at the graveside part of the service. He was a local director of missions. In that crowded space with no room to move, the man spoke for over twenty minutes. My legs were cramping, and I had an overwhelming desire to be away from the crowd. I am not claustrophobic as a rule, but this situation was stressful enough to make me think about it. The time finally came to lower the coffin into the ground.

What I saw next truly moved me. Once the coffin was safely in the bottom of the grave, the villagers began to cover it with dirt. They only had rudimentary tools for the task: a worn out shovel and an old pickaxe. The men literally fought each other for the right to take a turn with the tools to move dirt over the top of the coffin. No one man was allowed to work more than thirty seconds or a minute at the most. I figured out that it was considered an honor to help bury the loved one of the grieving family. Each man who loved his hurting neighbor wanted his turn at contributing to the completion of the task. I suppose that fifteen or twenty different men took turns moving the dirt into the grave. Not a single one of them was allowed a second turn. It only took five minutes or less to cover the grave.

The crowd began to disperse, and I was taken back to my hotel for the evening. I tried to share my experience with my church members, but words could not adequately describe the intensity of the day. Waves of emotion flooded over me as I tried to verbalize my feelings. I cried almost uncontrollably over a girl I'd never seen until they opened her casket the day of her funeral. We prayed for that family and the crowd who heard the gospel that day.

David, the Kenyan pastor, explained to me another tradition of his country concerning ministry to a grieving family. The people who attended the service were expected to gather at the same home on the third day after the funeral. They were expected to bring gifts of food, money, clothing, or other things the family might need. A collection basket was placed in front of the home for people to deposit their love gifts. I was afforded a special privilege: David asked the mother and father of the girl to meet with me prior to the formal meeting time with the rest of the guests.

As I sat down with this hurting couple, I prayed for the right words to say to them. Once again I expressed my deepest sympathy to them. They were gracious and thanked me for my words at their daughter's funeral. I could not help but think about my own two daughters, my youngest being about the same age as their girl. I struggled to imagine their feelings. I wondered what they were going through. I explained to them that I believed there was hope for them to see their daughter again. She had been a student at a local Christian school and was a professing believer in Jesus Christ. I shared the plan of salvation and had the sweet privilege of hearing both of them pray to receive Christ as their personal Lord and Savior. I gave them some money with the hope it would truly meet some need in their lives.

My mission trip to Africa was memorable, to say the least. I don't know why God ordained that I would preach the funeral message of a young girl in an African village. I don't believe it was a coincidence. My strongest conviction is that the Lord allowed this to happen to open up more opportunities for me to share His love with people. In the days following the funeral, the local people greeted me as the one who preached the message at the girl's service. I had a degree of credibility I would not have had otherwise. There was a connection and an acceptance that could not have come in any other way. I marvel at God's ability to bring life out of death.

Suggested Outlines

This chapter may prove to be the most helpful part of this book. I am including a few of my sermon outlines for your consideration. I have no delusions of grandeur in my soul. These are simple, straightforward outlines I have used in many situations. Some of the "explanation" sections of the message (the first paragraph under each point title) are adapted from various commentaries. The "application" section (the next paragraph) is of my own creation. I have tried to take out personal names from these outlines. The language gets a little stifled because I tried to be user friendly for either a male or a female. Feel free to use them, change them, or ignore them. Some outlines are more generic and will work fine in most situations. Others are geared toward more specific situations, such as the funeral of someone you did not know personally.

I have arranged the outlines in broad categories. Some deal with Christians who die in our congregations and we have no doubt about their eternity. Another group of sermons is directed toward families. The final group of outlines addresses difficult, funerals such as the death of children, those who suffered long illnesses, a total stranger, and those who died suddenly or tragically.

Funeral Outlines for Christians

It is important to keep in mind that funeral services and messages often focus on the living rather than the dead. This outline attempts to reassure the grieving family while reminding them to call upon the Lord for their strength.

Call on the Lord
Jeremiah 33:1-3

I. Regardless of Your Circumstances (v. 1)

Jeremiah is still in the courtyard of the guard when the Lord speaks to him a second time. He is a prisoner of war, held against his will in a foreign land. Jeremiah was a God-called prophet who spoke the Word of God to the people. Even with his privileged position in life, he still had to endure challenging times and circumstances.[1]

No matter what you are facing in life's journey, you can call upon the Lord. Whether it is fighting the enemy on the field of battle or fighting disease in your body, you can call on the Lord, and He will be there to strengthen and encourage you. Your loved one understood this throughout the journey of his/her life. He/she looked to the Lord, in good times and tough times, to be his/her strength and helper.

---

1   F.B. Huey, The New American Commentary, Jeremiah, Lamentations (Nashville, Tennessee: Broadman Press, 1993), 297-298.

II. He Is Able (v. 2)

Even though Jeremiah knew the Lord, God spoke and reminded His prophet of who He was. The name "Lord" here means "he exists" or "he causes to exist." The language is that of the creation story. God was reminding Jeremiah that the same God who had the power to create this world has the power to meet Jeremiah's needs.[2]

I believe that this brother/sister told us in life that his/her God is able, and I believe that if he/she could communicate to us from heaven, he/she would tell us the same thing. The Lord is the strength upon which you can depend in life and in death. God is taking care of this good man/woman now and forever.

III. God Knows (v. 3)

This verse is a remarkable reminder that God's knowledge far exceeds ours and that He is always ready to hear our appeals. This invitation from the Lord suggests that divine revelation becomes reality when it is sought. The word "unsearchable" means "inaccessible" or "impregnable." It can be used to describe a fortified city. God is describing matters so far beyond human insight that they require divine revelation.[3]

When we call upon the Lord, He never comes up short or fails to meet us right where we are. We will never ask Him a question that He cannot answer. He is the omniscient God. This person understood this fact in the journey of his/her life. He/her always remembered that God knew more than he/she did. Now, as he/she is in glory, can you imagine the things he/she is soaking in as he/she lives in God's uninterrupted presence in a perfect place called heaven?

---

2   Ibid.
3   Ibid.

More than one family has requested the "Lord's Prayer" as a text for the message at the funeral. I still prefer to call this the "Model Prayer," but I don't argue with people about it.

What God Wants
Matthew 6:9–13

I. Desire Him (vv. 9–10)

God wants us to view Him as personal and caring but holy and sovereign all at the same time. To ask for His kingdom to come is to ask that the messianic kingdom of Christ be extended here on earth. It is a prayer asking God to accomplish His will here on earth in the same way it is now accomplished in heaven. It is a way to tell the Lord that we want Him and His glory more than anything else on this earth.[4]

A child of God who has experienced His saving grace through faith in Jesus desires to know more and more of the Lord. God places within us a hunger and thirst to draw closer and closer to Him. He/she was that kind of person. He/she loved God in this life and desired to know Him more. Now he/she is in His very presence for all eternity.

---

4   D.A. Carson, The Expositor's Bible Commentary, Volume 8, (Grand Rapids, Michigan: Zondervan Publishing House, 1984), 169-174.

II. Trust Him (v. 11)

The last petitions of this prayer deal with our needs. "Bread" is a term to cover all food. The focus of this verse is on one day at a time. It is a recognition that all sustenance for our lives comes from God. All the good things we enjoy in this life come from the hand of God.[5]

The truth is you can trust God in life, and you can trust Him in death. God is faithful and true. Every day that you live, you can count on the Lord to meet your needs and see you through. Your loved one did just that. He/she trusted God with his/her salvation, and he/she trusted Him with every day he/she lived.

III. Forgiveness (v. 12)

These last three petitions are linked, as if to say daily food is not enough; we also need forgiveness of sin and deliverance from temptation. The "debts" described here are most certainly spiritual debts to God. A person who has experienced God's forgiving grace will most certainly be willing to extend that same forgiveness to others.[6]

Man's greatest need is forgiveness. Our sins cause us to fall short of God's glory and righteous requirements. Only in Jesus Christ do we find the grace and forgiveness we need to have eternal life. Our friend experienced that forgiveness in his/her life.

---

5   Ibid.
6   Ibid.

IV. Seek His Strength (v. 13)3

God does not tempt anyone. This means "don't abandon us to our own temptation." It is a plea that recognizes that we don't have the spiritual strength necessary to live like God wants us to live. Only through Jesus can we live like we should.[7]

God was the strength of this person's life. Now, He is his/her eternal glory as he/she is at His throne, worshiping Him with all the others who have gone before him/her. God is the strength that sees us through this life, and His strength keeps us safe for all of eternity.

---

7   Ibid.

Most of us know what the phrase "class clown" means. Perhaps you were that person in your school. Church congregations often have one or more of these cheerful souls who make everyone around them laugh. This message came out of my experience with such a man. This fellow was one of the funniest men I ever knew. He lived up into his nineties and was still pretty ornery when the Lord called him home. You could not think of this man without getting a smile on your face. I felt it necessary to reflect his joy and demeanor in the message. The Bible teaches us that laughter does good, like medicine. I think it is appropriate, at times, for there to be laughter in a funeral service. We laughed at this man's service as we remembered his wit and good humor.

Cheerful
Proverbs 15:13, 15

I. Seen in the Face (v. 13)

The emotional condition of a person has an obvious effect on body and soul. Joy is inspiring and expressed by a cheerful face, but heartache is depressing and crushes the spirit. The words here stress the pain and depression with a note of despair. A broken spirit is expressed by a sad face, but a cheerful face shows a courageous spirit.

You didn't have to be around this man/woman very long to recognize a cheerful face. He/she could bring a smile to others around him/her almost immediately. He/she had a great sense of humor and a good-natured spirit that shined through in every encounter. I've seen an entire room full of people laughing because of his/her cheerful spirit.[8]

---
8   Allen P. Ross, The Expositor's Bible Commentary, Volume 5, (Grand Rapids, Michigan: Zondervan Publishing House, 1991), 996.

II. Flows from Within (v. 15)

Life can be delightful or difficult, depending on one's circumstances and disposition. The contrast in this verse is between the "oppressed" and the "cheerful heart." The writer recommends the cheerful frame of mind, for the image of the feast signifies enjoyment of life's blessings.[9]

The reason this friend could be so much fun on the outside was because of what he/she possessed on the inside. He/she had given his/her heart to Christ, and his/her life was filled with joy. That joy overflowed in his/her laughter, teasing, and relationships with others around him/her. Even when he/she didn't feel well, he/she still managed to make jokes and have fun. He/she was a true blessing, and we will miss him/her until we get to see him/her again in glory.

---

9   Ibid.

It is far more pleasant to preach the funeral of a faithful church member than an unfaithful one. Most pastors can name many people who faithfully come to church and worship wholeheartedly on a consistent basis. It is gratifying to see people understand the importance of genuine worship. It is moving to witness them worshiping God with their entire being.

Praising God
Psalm 100

I. Worship (vv. 1–2)

The whole earth is summoned to "shout for joy to the Lord. The nations must recognize who the Lord is: He is Yahweh, by whose grace and blessings His people exist. The nations are invited to sing hymns to the Lord and worship Him. The invitation is a free offer. The submission to God's rule comes out of a heart response of joy and gratitude for His covenant promises. The "gladness" reflects the joy in living in harmony with the Creator, Redeemer, and King.[10]

This dear loved one spent his/her lifetime worshiping God with his/her heart, soul, mind, and strength. He/she was the kind who committed himself/herself to the things of God: Sunday school, intercessory prayer, worship, and service to his/her king. He/she got it right.

---

10 William A. VanGemeren, The Expositor's Bible Commentary, Volume 5, (Grand Rapids, Michigan: Zondervan Publishing House, 1991), 639-640.

II. Confession (v. 3)

The word translated "know" means to make a confession. True worshipers confess Him as covenant Lord, their only true God. In addition they confess accountability to Him and their privileged position (sheep of His pasture).[11]

The reason we know this brother/sister is in heaven today is because he/she confessed Jesus as his/her Lord and Savior in his/her life. If you have been born twice, you only have to die once. He/she is at home with his/her Lord.

III. God Is Faithful (vv. 4–5)

The communal confession arouses another invocation to give thanks to the Lord. This verse stresses the communal act of worship. They come with thanksgiving and with praise. God is good and full of love. God remains faithful to His people because He has covenanted to do so.[12]

We trust God. We can take Him at His word because He will not lie to us. God promised to prepare a place for His children. He promised eternal life to all who would accept His Son as Savior. Your dear loved one not only enjoyed God's faithfulness throughout his/her lifetime, but now he/she is experiencing it face to face.

---

11 Ibid.
12 Ibid.

The following is another example of an outline designed for the funeral of a faithful, hardworking church member. It looks to the kind of person that you wish all your church members were. Selfishly, you wish these kind could stay around a little longer because of their deep commitment and effectiveness in the kingdom.

A Faithful Life
2 Timothy 2:3–7

I. Stand Up and Be Counted (vv. 3–4)

Paul's appeal to "endure hardship" means literally to suffer together with someone; it has the idea to "join the ranks of those who bear suffering." It is the idea of standing up and being counted for the cross. The soldier was concerned to obey his commander twenty-four hours a day, and Paul wanted Timothy to display the same zeal in his commitment to the Lord. To get "involved in civilian affairs" called for Timothy not to be absorbed in merely living or existing. Paul is describing single-minded devotion to Christ throughout life.[13]

There can be little doubt that this child of God was a "stand up and be counted" kind of man/woman. He/she was not ashamed to be called a Christian. He/she was willing to stand up for what he/she believed in and willing to take any trouble that might come as a result.

---

13 Thomas D. Lea, Hayne P. Griffin, Jr., The New American Commentary, 1,2 Timothy, Titus, (Nashville, Tennessee: Broadman Press, 1992), 202-206.

II. Stay Committed (v. 5)

Paul used the picture of the athlete to illustrate the importance of complete devotion and stamina in Christian living. Performing as an athlete demands a commitment to a regimen of training and to the rules for the game. Paul implied that the Christian athlete could expect suffering, but he also held out the promise of a prize for the committed devotee.[14]

Throughout your loved one's life, he/she stayed committed to the things he/she loved: Christ, work, family, friends, and convictions. He/she was committed to his/her family. He/she was committed to hard work. He/she was committed to the Lord.

III. Hard Work Pays Off (vv. 6–7)

Paul used the analogy of the farmer to show that the one who works hard has the first claim on the fruits of the work. The phrase "to receive a share of the crops" is not an appeal for a diligent worker to receive an adequate salary; it promises a spiritual reward from God for a job devotedly done. The main thought is that labor, discipline, and striving are the portions of him who would succeed in any enterprise, be he soldier, athlete, or farmer. Paul urged Timothy to ponder these illustrations and God would give him insight into their meaning.[15]

This one was a hard worker. It paid off in his/her career, and it paid off in life. His/her faith in Jesus and his/her commitment to the Lord now results in an eternal reward that will not fade away. Your loved one is home with the Lord. He/she will enjoy that reward forever.

---

14 Ibid.
15 Ibid.

Here is another simple outline to preach at a Christian's funeral. It is a straightforward reminder of the hope we have in Christ and the power of His resurrection.

Living Hope
1 Peter 1:3–9

I. Our Inheritance (vv. 3–5)

The new birth that Christians experience is the work of the Holy Spirit. The Christian has a "living hope" because Jesus has been raised from the dead. Our hope is in an inheritance that can never perish, spoil, or fade. This inheritance is kept (perfect tense) or reserved by God for His people in heaven. God's people are described as "the ones being guarded," which is the continued activity of God. Our job, in the meantime, is to exercise faith in the One who holds our inheritance for us.[16]

The greatest inheritance man could hope for is eternal life in heaven. God's Word makes it clear that this is the promise for those who are born again by the power of God's Spirit. It is not something we work toward. Just like you don't work to earn an inheritance from your parents, we can't earn our heavenly inheritance; it is God's gift.

---

16 Edwin A. Blum, The Expositor's Bible Commentary, Volume 12, (Grand Rapids, Michigan: Zondervan Publishing House, 1981), 220-221.

II. Our Faith (vv. 6–7)

Peter gives a reference to the anticipation of the future deliverance we will enjoy when God calls us home to heaven. We can rejoice over the fact that heaven will be our home one day. In the meantime, we will suffer grief and difficulty in this life. The language points out that the suffering of this life is brief in comparison to eternity. When gold is refined, its impurities are removed by a fiery process. Gold belongs to the realm of this perishing world. Faith is more valuable because it lasts longer and reaches beyond this temporal order. Faith is purified by the tests of life. God will bless faith tested by fire.[17]

Life has no guarantees of being pain free. In fact, the Bible makes it clear that just the opposite will be true: life on this earth comes with pain and disappointment. In the midst of the strife, we can hold on to our hope in Jesus and rise above life's circumstances with a strong faith in the One who will deliver us one day.

III. Our Salvation (vv. 8–9)

"For you are receiving" gives the reason for our rejoicing in the midst of life's struggles. This life is temporary; heaven is eternal. Those saved by faith through Jesus can look forward with great joy for what lies ahead.[18]

When you know Jesus as your personal Lord and Savior, you don't have to be afraid of death. Instead of seeing death as the end, you come to realize that it is the beginning. The hope of heaven is found in a personal relationship with Christ. Those who put their faith and trust in the Lord will receive their eternal inheritance one day.

---

17 Ibid.
18 Ibid.

Every one of these sermon outlines carries a strong memory for me. There was a man with a long-term, incurable disease in my church. He tried several experimental treatments, but nothing worked. I watched God do a powerful work in this man's life. He became more open and expressive as death approached. He found new release to tell others how he truly felt about them. His words were like soothing waters in a barren desert land. He blessed my life with his words of encouragement. I witnessed him blessing several other members of our congregation with his words of edification. He would open up and share during our Wednesday night Bible study times. He said some of the most insightful, powerful things I've ever heard from a layman. God impressed the following message on my heart when this wonderful man passed away.

Ready to Go
Philippians 1:3–8

I. Deep Joy (vv. 3–6)

Paul's thanks is no stereotyped formula but the natural outflow from the heart of a deeply spiritual man. His thanksgiving was prompted by the joyous memory Paul had of his friends. Joy permeated his prayers as he prayed for their needs. Paul's deepest joy came through the relationship they shared in Christ. Paul was confident that God would continue to work in their lives until Jesus came again. The "good work" he mentions is a reference to their salvation, which began at their conversion.[19]

---

19 Homer A. Kent, Jr., The Expositor's Bible Commentary, Volume 11, (Grand Rapids, Michigan: Zondervan Publishing House, 1978), 105-106.

This man/woman loved all of you deeply. These last days of his/her life were mainly focused on you and your needs. He/she was a glowing example of selflessness and exhibited a servant's heart.

II. Shared Journey (v. 7)

The Philippians had become partners with Paul in his imprisonment and legal obligations. They were not afraid to be identified with the apostle, even though he was in jail. To say they were in his heart meant more than mere emotions or sentiment, but the essence of consciousness and personality. They were willing to stick with Paul through the challenges of his most difficult days.[20]

As your loved one endured these last few months of his/her life, the family stuck with him/her through it all. Life has no guarantees, and we must realize that we will all face the tough times as well as the happy times. I know it was a labor of love, but thank you for sharing in the journey with him/her and staying by his/her side right up to the moment God called him/her home.

III. Love of God (v. 8)

It was the indwelling Christ who was producing the fruit of love in Paul by the Holy Spirit and who thus enabled him to yearn for the Philippians' welfare with the compassion of the Lord.[21]

He/she loved all of you, not only with his/her own heart but also with the love of God he/she found in a personal relationship with Jesus Christ. His/her last conversation with me involved what

---

20 Ibid.
21 Ibid.

would happen to him/her when he/she died, but also his/her heart was burdened that all his/her family members know Christ as Savior and Lord of their lives.

Here is another simple outline that would work in most situations. This passage does lend itself to addressing the challenges most people face in the journey of life.

The Journey of Life
Psalm 66:8-20

I. Times of Trouble (vv. 8–12)

The fact is God allows all His children to go through times of testing and trial. Even Jesus went through many difficulties as He lived on this earth. The testing works much like the refining fires of the silversmith: the dross and tin are burned up and the pure ore is left. At times it feels like the trouble surrounds us on every side or like everybody is stepping on us. However, the Psalmist remembered that God had brought the children of Israel to a place of abundance. The same God who allowed them the struggles of Egypt also brought them into the land flowing with milk and honey.[22]

We can relate to the writer's review of life. All of us will have to endure times of trouble in this life: health issues, disappointments, pain, grief, and sorrow. However, those of us who have trusted Jesus as Savior understand that one day God will call us home and we will be delivered into God's heaven for all eternity. We hold on with hope and trust. Our friend has been delivered into a land that is fairer than day. No trouble touches him/her there.

---
22 Charles H. Spurgeon, The Treasury of David, Volume 2, (Peadbody, Massachusetts: Hendrickson Publishers, n.d.), 110-114.

II. Love for God (vv. 13–15)

The writer felt so indebted to God that he broke out in a song of commitment. He promised to come into God's house with sacrifices and an attitude of worship. He wanted to give God his best because God deserved his best. As he realized all that the Lord had done for him and all He would do, the Psalmist wanted to praise, worship, and serve Him.[23]

There is no doubt that your loved one had a genuine love for the Lord. He/she spoke often of his/her thanks to God for all the Lord had done for him/her. He/she had a sweet love for the Lord.

III. A Clear Testimony (vv. 16–20)

The Psalmist was not afraid to tell others about his love for the Lord. He testified about God's goodness and mercy in his life. He praised God for loving him and hearing his prayers.[24]

This man/woman gave clear testimony of God's working in his/her life. There was no doubt that he/she loved the Lord and thanked God for saving his/her soul. His/her testimony has touched many lives; it is still touching lives today. He/she is now face to face with the Jesus he/she loved so much; he/she is able to thank the Lord in person.

---

23 Ibid.
24 Ibid.

This last outline is as generic as it gets. I will confess that I go to this one fairly often, especially when called upon to preach the funeral of a total stranger. I use it if the family can give a clear testimony of the deceased's faith in Christ. It is my go-to message when I cannot find another one for the funeral service.

Funeral Message
Revelation 14:13

I. Death Is a Release

"Blessed are those who die in the Lord."

From our perspective here on earth, death is a horrible time of pain, sorrow, and separation. From heaven's perspective, death is a release from this life into God's glory. It is the door from the temporal to the eternal.

For Christians, death releases them to see God's glory face to face. They meet Jesus and see Him as He is. They enter into their eternal reward. God sees this transition as a precious sight because He welcomes His children into His glorious presence. When you stop and recognize all the implications of the death of a believer, you begin to understand why Jesus would call the event a blessing.

II. Death Is Rest

"They will rest from their labor."

As a Christian passes from this life to the next, there will be no more the struggle of this life with its ups and downs and disappointments. There will be no more pain, suffering, or sorrow in heaven and no more separation, good-byes, or times of fear.

Heaven also marks the end of the labor of this life. In glory, there will no longer be the endless, daily grind of labor. There will be no more need for work in the Lord's fields because we enter into His magnificent presence. In heaven, the Christian enjoys an eternity of rest and reward for faithful labor done below.

III. Death Cannot Stop Results

"Their deeds will follow them."

The impact of a faithful life lived for the glory of God does not stop at the time a person dies. That impact carries beyond that time. A faithful life can touch countless other lives with its witness and testimony. There are family members who carry on beliefs and values instilled by their loved ones who have gone on to be with the Lord. The love expressed by that faithful life has continuing impact as it is passed on to others. Communities are blessed by a Christian's life through the kindness and integrity. Those memories live on long after the funeral service is over.

Funeral Outlines for Families

Many men are identified by their role as a father. It is a strong biblical model, as we are taught that God longs to be our Father. This message attempts to celebrate the gift of a godly father.

Faithful Father
1 Kings 2:1-4

I. Influence (vv. 1–2a)

As David approached the time of his death, he had a desire to pass along some instructions to Solomon by giving him a "charge." This is a beautiful scene of a faithful father giving expression to a heartfelt desire to influence a son by passing along some of the wisdom gained through life's journey.[25]

Your loved one influenced your lives. Whether he did it with words, like David here, or by his example, this man invested his life in yours. There are characteristics, habits, opinions, practices, and countless other ways he had influence on you. You carry a part of his love and life in yours today.

---

25 Paul R. House, The New American Commentary, 1,2 Kings, (Nashville, Tennessee: Broadman & Holman Publishers, 1995), 96.

II. Insight (vv. 2b–3)

David shares insight with Solomon that he gained from living life. David had learned, through life's hard knocks, that the best approach to life is to follow God wholeheartedly. David had learned that he could trust God, even when it didn't make sense. He knew that obeying the Lord and honoring Him with his commitment was the best way to live. David knew that while he stayed close to God and lived a holy life, the Lord would be glorified. David wanted his son to live such a life.[26]

Your loved one placed his faith and trust in Jesus for his salvation. That is always the best decision any of us can make in life. Any time we honor the Lord with our choices, actions, and approach to life, God is pleased.

III. Impact (vv. 3b–4)

To carry out the thought about his insight for living, David reminded Solomon that God would bless a life of faithfulness. The most successful life is not measured by this world's standards; it is measured by God's approval. To live a life rich with God's blessings is to be truly successful.[27]

Your loved one had such blessings in his life. His family was very important to him. You were a part of God's blessing in his life, and he was a part of God's blessing in yours. That is true success.

---

26 Ibid.
27 Ibid.

This outline was written for a wonderful church member who truly loved the Lord. He was quiet in his spirit but faithful in his devotion to Christ. His life spoke volumes to everyone who knew him.

A True Gentleman
Ephesians 4:1–3

I. A Worthy Life (v. 1)

What Paul urges is that the Ephesians may lead the sort of life that matches their Christian calling. "Worthy" is literally *"bringing up the other beam of the scales."* Paul is insisting that there should be a balance between profession and practice. True Christians will always seek to do what is most in keeping with their vocation.[28]

Many people profess to be Christians, but the real evidence is more clearly seen in the lifestyle of the individual. This man lived out his faith in a way that was evident to all who knew him. His was a "worthy" life, according to the Word of God.

II. Filled with God's Graces (v. 2)

Paul specifies four graces that evidence this essential proportion between calling and character: humility, gentleness, patience, and forbearance. These are all qualities necessary for good relations in the Christian community and beyond. Humility is the opposite of the high-mindedness of the lost. Gentleness is considerateness, which includes

---

28 A. Skevington Wood, The Expositor's Bible Commentary, Volume 11, (Grand Rapids, Michigan: Zondervan Publishing House, 1978), 54-55.

the element of restraint so that it denotes controlled strength. Patience describes the reluctance to avenge wrongs. Bearing with one another means to put up with others' faults because you recognize you have faults yourself.[29]

A true believer will be filled with clear evidence of God's power and grace. Those Christ-like qualities will flow out of the believer's life. He had these qualities in his life. I think the term "gentleness" best describes him. It does not mean weakness but controlled strength. If you knew this man, you knew the Lord's strength was in his life.

III. Completely Committed (v. 3)

The absence of those qualities mentioned in verse two may jeopardize Christian unity, so Paul presses his readers to maintain oneness in Christ. He is describing a profound oneness made possible by God's Spirit. God's peace and love will abound in lives committed to His will and way of life.[30]

This brother was completely committed to God's will and way of life. Consequently, the Lord's peace and love were clearly evident in his life and approach to others. Now, in heaven, our friend is in the presence of pure peace and love.

---

29 Ibid.
30 Ibid.

Most of my sermonic work is exegetical. Occasionally I will write one that is more topical in nature. This sermon grew out of a story I heard from the family of a woman who passed away in our community. They told me how their home was a gathering place for the neighborhood. Children and adults alike would congregate on this woman's front porch. She always had refreshments for the kids. No one was ever turned away. There was no such thing as a stranger at her house. New people simply became a part of the fellowship. As I prayed about a message to encourage the family and honor this woman's life, I thought of that special place where Jesus often went to get away from the demands of ministry.

A Home of Love
Luke 10:38

Introduction

Bethany was a significant place in the life and ministry of the Lord Jesus. One key part of that place was the home of His friends, Mary, Martha, and Lazarus. It is interesting to study all that happened in and around Bethany and compare it to our own lives today.

I. A Place of Preparation

The Bible tells us that John the Baptist did his baptizing around the area of Bethany. It would have also been the area where he would have shared his message to prepare the way for the Lord. Jesus went to Bethany before and after His triumphal entry, where the people cried out "Hosanna" to Him. At the home of His close friends, Mary anointed Jesus with expensive perfume before He was crucified.

As you think about your mom's home, it too was a place of preparation for your lives. There you learned many of life's lessons that you still refer to till this day. The love, influence, and impact of your mom in your lives helped prepare you to live your life each day.

II. A Place of Peace

The Bible makes it clear that Jesus went to Bethany often as He went about His ministry among the people of His day. Apparently it was a place of refuge and rest for the Lord as He faced the demands placed upon Him.

Home can and should generate those kinds of feelings in all of us. It has little to do with the physical location of the dwelling and everything to do with the love, security, acceptance, and peace we enjoy with our loved ones. This lady's home was such a place, not only for you but also for many who entered there.

III. A Place of Power

Bethany is also the place where Jesus raised His friend Lazarus from the dead. The Bible also shares that it was near Bethany that Jesus ascended back to heaven out of the sight of the disciples.

One of the greatest things that can happen in our homes is to learn about God and His love for us through Jesus Christ. The Lord's power and grace make a home a powerful place in our lives. Hang on to those good things you learned from the wonderful home of love you were blessed with as you grew up.

Many funeral messages for women come from Proverbs 31. There is nothing wrong with preaching from that famous passage. I have had family members tell me, however, that they preferred I not preach from those verses because so many sermons have come from there. This sermon offers one of many possibilities for a meaningful message to share at a woman's funeral.

A Mother's Love
John 19:25-27

I. Near the Cross (v. 25)

John's gospel tells us many details of the crucifixion scene because he was the only one of the twelve apostles who dared to be there. Prior to this verse, we are told of the Roman soldiers gambling for Jesus's garment. These women who loved the Lord are a stark contrast to the rest of the scene around Jesus's crucifixion. These ladies were near the cross because they loved Jesus and honored Him. They had a front-row seat to the greatest event recorded in history: the death of God's Son for the sins of mankind.[31]

The soldiers and these women paint a picture of all humanity when it comes to considering Jesus's death on the cross and what it means. Some ignore the fact of His atoning death and miss heaven; others come to the message of the cross with conviction and devotion and receive the sweet gift of eternal life. This lady was one of those sweet women who came to the message of the cross in the right way: she accepted Jesus as her sacrifice for her sins.

---

31 Merrill C. Tenney, The Expositor's Bible Commentary, Volume 9, (Grand Rapids, Michigan: Zondervan Publishing House, 1981), 182.

II. Jesus Took Care of Her (vv. 26–27)

Jesus's tender concern for Mary in the hour of His mortal agony illustrates His true humanity and compassion. Jesus fulfilled His family responsibility as the oldest Son by arranging Mary's care with John, the beloved disciple. It is truly a beautiful picture of grace and compassion as the Lord is weighted down with the sins of the world while He still cared for His dear mother.[32]

Those who put their faith and trust in Jesus not only receive the gift of eternal life but also His tender compassion and care. Your loved one had a sweet walk with the Lord in her life. She served Him with faithfulness and gladness on a daily basis. She loved being in God's house with God's people. More than anything else, she desired that all of her family enjoy the same peace and joy in Jesus that she did.

---

32 Ibid.

Funeral Outlines for Difficult Situations

Likely you will minister to people who suffer through long-term illness. I find that the caregivers often struggle more than the patients. The following outline was written with a view of a faithful spouse and family members who stood beside their loved one throughout a lengthy illness. It is important to honor such people and acknowledge their devotion.

Tender Care
Mark 2:1-12

I. You Did All You Could (vv. 1-4)

This was likely the home of Peter and Andrew. The crowds flocked to this house in hopes of seeing Jesus perform more miracles. However, Jesus wasn't performing miracles that day; He was preaching the gospel. The houses of that region and era would have been single-room dwellings with flat roofs that were accessible by an outside stair. The roof would have been made of wooden beams, with thatch and dried mud. These four men tore a hole in the roof in order to gain access to Jesus.[33]

One has to admire the tenacity of these four friends. The simple obstacle of a crowded doorway was not enough to keep them from their mission: to give their friend the best care possible. Family and friends, you have done the same for this dear one. You did whatever needed to be done in order to minister to his/her needs. Thank you for your good example to the rest of us.

---

33 Walter W. Wessel, The Expositor's Bible Commentary, Volume 8, (Grand Rapids, Michigan: Zondervan Publishing House, 1984), 632-634.

II. Forgiven By Christ (vv. 5–11)

Jesus recognized their ingenuity and persistence as faith. The Lord forgave the man's sins instead of healing his lameness. Forgiveness was actually the greater need. The critics were there to try to ensnare Christ on some theological point. For anyone but God to claim to forgive sin was blasphemy. They failed to recognize Jesus for who He was. The Lord knew their thoughts and questioned them. Jesus healed the paralytic and verified His claim to grant forgiveness. As sure as actual healing followed, "Get up," so actual forgiveness followed, "Your sins are forgiven."[34]

We all desire to see our loved ones free from pain and suffering. Praying for healing is proper for people of faith. However, we need to remember that our greatest need is not the healing of some physical condition but the forgiveness of our sins through a personal relationship with Jesus Christ. Thank God this dear man/woman experienced that in his/her lifetime.

III. The Ultimate Healing (v. 12)

The cure was instantaneous, and the paralytic walked out of the house. The emphasis in this account is on the forgiveness and not the healing.[35]

In the case of your loved one, we didn't get the privilege of seeing the miracle, but I assure you that when he/she drew his/her last breath, he/she walked into eternity to a reward awaiting him from the Lord. It is unlike anything we've ever seen in this world. There, he/she is healed ultimately and completely. Never again will he/she struggle for breath or have any pain whatsoever. God has blessed him/her with eternal healing and eternal life.

---

34 Ibid.
35 Ibid.

This outline is a very generic one that will apply to any Christian's life. This one also works well for the funeral of someone who has suffered a long illness. It is a good reminder of the promises we have from the Bible of the hope of eternal life.

We Will Overcome
2 CORINTHIANS 4:7–18

I. Relying on Jesus (vv. 7–12)

Paul is describing the paradox of a sinner saved by God's grace in Jesus. Our human lives, compared to the immeasurable value of the gospel, are nearly worthless. Paul used four vivid statements to illustrate his weaknesses and God's power in preserving him through it all. *"Hard pressed on every side,"* but never completely cornered. *"Perplexed,"* but never at his wit's end. *"Persecuted,"* but not left alone. *"Struck down,"* but not permanently grounded. In all the challenges Paul faced, he made it through because of Jesus.[36]

This dear one experienced many difficulties in his/her lifetime. He/she faced great challenges, but he/she made it through. How? By relying on Jesus, just like Paul did a long time ago. The grace of Jesus is sufficient to see us through life's journey. This friend was a testimony to that grace.

---

36 Murray J. Harris, The Expositor's Bible Commentary, Volume 10, (Grand Rapids, Michigan: Zondervan Publishing House, 1976), 342-345.

II. Resurrection Power (vv. 13–15)

Paul was able to discharge his ministry, even in the midst of suffering, because he believed faith cannot remain silent and that Christ's resurrection guarantees the resurrection of all believers. Paul gladly shared his faith because it was the foundation of his life and source of his confidence. He understood that the fact that Jesus had been resurrected from the dead guaranteed his own resurrection from the dead.[37]

As believers in Christ, we share the same confidence today. Because Jesus is alive, we too shall live eternally. Your loved placed his/her faith and trust in Jesus, and now he/she is home with Him forever. One day, at the second coming, his/her body will be raised up and transformed brand new and will be equipped to live for all eternity. In the meantime, to be absent from the body is to be present with the Lord.

III. Remembering All This Is Temporary (vv. 16–18)

As Paul went about his duties for the Lord, his body grew weaker, but his spirit grew stronger. Each day, God gave Paul the strength to make it through. He understood that all the hardships he endured were momentary, but the glory he would experience in heaven would last forever. So he chose to focus his thoughts and life on the eternal glory and not the temporary struggles of life.[38]

As born-again believers, we must take Paul's example to heart. It is easy to focus on all the hard times in life and be discouraged. Remember that all the pain and heartache of this life cannot and will not follow us into eternity. Your loved one has experienced that glorious transition from the temporary to the eternal. He/she is not hurting or suffering in any way!

---

37 Ibid.
38 Ibid.

People are often critical of pastors who preach the gospel at a funeral service. I think it ridiculous to criticize a man of God for sharing the most important message anyone will ever hear. I understand the fear of the preacher "giving an altar call" at the memorial service of a loved one. However, you may experience what I have time and time again: the church member and or the family make a specific request that the gospel be shared and an invitation given. If the person who died was an effective soul winner in your church, it makes sense that he or she would want you to remember him or her by doing what they he or she loved to do: share Jesus. The outline from 2 Peter 3:9 offers the opportunity to be evangelistic while celebrating a person's faithful life.

He Loves Everyone
2 PETER 3:9

I. Great Misunderstanding

"The Lord is not slow in keeping his promise, as some understand slowness."

There were critics in Peter's day who scoffed at the notion that Jesus was returning one day and a new kingdom was going to be established. People were critical because it hadn't happened yet. They questioned God and those who preached the message. Because they did not understand it, they were critical of it.[39]

---

39 Edwin A. Blum, The Expositor's Bible Commentary, Volume 12, (Grand Rapids, Michigan: Zondervan Publishing House, 1981), 285-286.

Unfortunately, there are many today who are still critical of Christianity and the things of God. They don't understand it, so they criticize it and question it. When you have a personal relationship with Jesus Christ, you won't always understand all that comes in life's journey, but you will learn that you can trust the Lord in all things. This dear one did just this. He/she did not complain about his/her illness; he/she only praised God.

II. The Truth of the Matter

"He is patient with you, not wanting anyone to perish, but everyone to come to repentance."

God's "delay" in sending Jesus back is gracious; it is not caused by inability or indifference. God's time plan is influenced by His patience. His patience is directed toward you. So wonderful is God's love toward mankind that He would have them all to be saved and is of His own self prepared to bestow salvation on the lost. Every day that Jesus tarries His second coming is evidence that God is patient and wants everyone to hear about salvation through a personal relationship with His Son, Jesus Christ.[40]

Our friend had this same spirit as he/she lay on a bed in his/her home facing certain death. More than anything else, he/she desired that the gospel be shared here today. He/she shared that if there was one person who hadn't accepted Jesus, that person needed to hear the truth at his/her funeral service. He/she wanted that person to do more than just hear it; his/her prayer was that everyone in attendance at his/her funeral service be born again.

---

40 Ibid.

The following outline addresses the issue of a rebellious son. You will likely perform the service for a son or daughter who rebelled against his or her family and God. It attempts to point out the love in spite of the pain.

For the Love of a Son
2 SAMUEL 18:5, 32-33

I. Unconditional Love (v. 5)

As the armies of Israel went out to battle, the primary thought on the mind of King David was about his son. As king, David was the commander in chief of the army. His last instruction to his commanders related to his son, Absalom. David's words give clear evidence of his unconditional love for his son despite Absalom's choices that broke his father's heart.[41]

Children are one of the greatest joys of this life. While they can be the greatest source of joy, they can also be the source of our greatest hurts as well. However, no matter what happens in life, parents still love their children. What parents desire more than anything else is for their children to be well and whole.

---

41 Ronald F. Youngblood, The Expositor's Bible Commentary, Volume 13, (Grand Rapids, Michigan: Zondervan Publishing House, 1992), 1018.

II. Primary Concern (v. 32)

As the battle was over, the reports came to David. More than the issue of victory or defeat, David was concerned about Absalom. It is obvious that the king's primary focus was on his son rather than the condition of the army, the nation, or anything else.[42]

In the course of this life, those closest to us are the primary focus of our experience. More than world issues or even personal comforts, our concern most often focuses on those we love the most. We want to know their status; we want to know that they are all right. All other considerations are secondary compared to those we love the most.

III. A Broken Heart (v. 33)

David finally heard the news that he feared the most: Absalom had fallen on the field of battle. His reaction is understandable in light of his great love for his son. David was shaken and mourned intensely for his son. His cry was that of a parent's broken heart. His tears were those of a hurting father.[43]

When someone you love is hurting, you hurt. When someone passes away, it affects you deeply, especially when it happens suddenly or unexpectedly. Realize that your broken heart is a clear indicator of your deep love. Remember the promises of Scripture that help mend your broken heart. Remember the truth of Jesus's empty tomb and the promise of eternal life for all His children who trusted Him for their salvation.

---

42 Ibid, 1027-1028.
43 Ibid, 1028.

I have mentioned the difficulty of preaching at the funeral of a child. I find that a child's death impacts everyone involved. I have seen men who work in the funeral business break down and weep uncontrollably at a child's memorial service. I have had to ask God to control my own emotions as I stood over a tiny casket and looked into the eyes of the parents who were hurting so deeply from the death of their little one. There is a pain in the eyes of parents, especially mothers, who lose a child that will make your knees tremble. This outline looks at the story of the Shunammite woman who hosted the prophet Elisha in her home. Elisha desired to do something nice for her and discovered she had never had children. He prophesied that she would hold a son in her arms in about a year. The boy later died, and the woman was heartbroken.

A Time for Faith
2 Kings 4:8–37

I. Gift of a Child (vv. 8–17)

Elisha was seeking to establish himself as God's new prophet. His predecessor, Elijah, was well known. The woman in the story recognized Elisha as a "holy man of God." She convinced her husband that they ought to prepare a special room just for the prophet of God. Elisha wanted to reward her hospitality. It seemed she had everything she wanted except children, so Elisha promised her a son. The promise was fulfilled, even though her husband was old. The child was nothing short of a miracle.[44]

---

44 Paul R. House, The New American Commentary, 1,2 Kings, (Nashville, Tennessee: Broadman & Holman Publishers, 1995), 267-268.

The miracle of life can only come because of the power and blessing of God. *A child is a gift from God. All life is precious and is God's gift.* Your precious son/daughter was a special gift from God. Though there have certainly been difficult days, he/she brought you a great deal of joy and blessing. He/she was God's gift.

II. Power of Faith (vv. 8–17)

A crisis emerged when the boy felt pain in his head and died in his mother's lap. In response to her tragedy, this mother laid the boy in the prophet's room upstairs, traveled to Mt. Carmel where Elisha lived, clung to the prophet even though others tried to pull her away, and pleaded with Elisha by reminding him that she didn't ask for the blessing of a son (in other words, she was not selfish). All of her actions demonstrated her faith in God to meet her needs.[45]

The love that God gives a mother for her child will travel however many miles it takes; climb any mountain; cling to hope with determination; and argue and plead with every ounce of energy she has for her child. After she did all she could do in her own power and ability, she had to rely on faith. You have done all you could do for your son/daughter. You went the extra mile, stayed the course, and gave your all. Now, though it may seem difficult, you too must look to faith in God to see you through this dark hour.

---

45 Ibid.

III. Power of God (vv. 29–37)

Elisha went straight for the child, putting all others out and shutting the door. The prophet sought the Lord for the boy's life. His prayers were followed by prophetic actions. The mother waited outside the room as Elisha pleaded to God on behalf of the boy. As the boy was resurrected, he was reunited with his loving mother.[46]

There is no doubt that this was a true miracle of God. However, it is the exception and not the rule. Many children die and are not brought back to life. *However, I know of another son who died and came back to life as well. His name is Jesus. He is God's Son, and His death and resurrection is the greatest miracle of all time.* Faith in Jesus as Savior and Lord will provide you the promise and hope of eternal life. Children are innocent in the Lord until such time that they can recognize sin and wrongdoing, repent of their sins, and trust Jesus as their Savior. I believe your son/daughter is in heaven today. You can go there too if you put your faith and trust in Jesus to be your Savior.

---

46 Ibid.

I am including another message written for a baby's funeral. As I have mentioned before, these are the most painful to preach.

Jesus Loves the Children
Mark 10:13-16

I. Children Are Never a Waste of Tim e (vv. 13-14a)

Among Jews, it was customary to bring children to great men to have them blessed. Perhaps the disciples wanted to protect Jesus's privacy and shield Him from needless interruptions. Though their motives may have been commendable, they showed a lack of spiritual sensitivity here. Jesus was angry with the disciples when He realized what they were doing. He was upset that anyone would think children are unimportant.[47]

It has been often said that if it is important to the Lord, it ought to be important to us. Children are important to Jesus; He never looked upon them as a waste of His time or power. Jesus gladly welcomed the children, at any time, to love them and bless them. We can be reminded today of the uncertainty of life and the importance of taking the time to love our kids and pay attention to them. Yes, there are times when children can be an inconvenience, but God help us to never see them as a waste of time. Thank God for all of you who invested your lives in this little one's life.

---

47 Walter W. Wessel, The Expositor's Bible Commentary, Volume 18, (Grand Rapids, Michigan: Zondervan Publishing House, 1984), 713-714.

II. Children Set the Example for the Rest of Us (vv. 14b–15)

Jesus made a point to the disciples: children, in their receptivity and dependence upon others, exemplify the characteristics of those who possess God's kingdom. The kingdom of God is to be received as a little child receives.[48]

Childlike faith is a necessary quality for salvation, regardless of one's age. As kids understand, they need others to provide their basic needs every day, so a person must recognize that he cannot save himself. This little one had not yet come to that place of understanding all that salvation means. The Bible makes it clear that children are protected under the grace of God. David's baby who died in 2 Samuel went to be with the Lord. I believe this little one is with Jesus today.

III. Jesus Loves Our Children Even More than We Do (v. 16)

Jesus took the children into His arms—a striking act showing His love for them. The language here communicates the idea of blessing fervently with an intensive force. In other words, Jesus's deep, intense love for these children was overflowing through His expression of blessings on their lives.[49]

Jesus loves this child even more than we do. We might want to argue the point, but He is perfect and we are not. This baby is with Jesus now, in those same wonderful arms that held the children in this account, giving him/her an even greater blessing.

---

48 Ibid.
49 Ibid.

The first time you stand over the body of a total stranger, you may feel at a loss as what to say about that person. You may also encounter a situation where the one who passed away never attended church or showed commitment to Christ in his or her life. These are the most difficult funeral services of all. I've done more of them than I care to recall.

I use one outline I borrowed from a book put out by the Annuity Board many years ago. Paul Powell was president at that time and wrote a book called *Death from the Other Side*. In this excellent work is an outline from Job 1:20–21. Dr. Powell outlined the gift, the grief, and the grace that Job experienced. I have used this outline numerous times to speak of the life of a lost person.

Every life, regardless of that person's failure, could be considered a gift to someone who loved him or her. There is grief when someone we love dies. God's grace is the only way we can make it through our sorrow. In addition to Dr. Powell's sermon, I wrote the following to focus on a person's good name and reputation. It can be a delicate situation to speak of someone you know did not go to church or follow the Lord. This sermon from Proverbs attempts to focus on some positive aspects of a person's life without delving in too deeply in the matters of eternity.

A Good Name
Proverbs 22:1

I. Great Riches

"More desirable than great riches ..."

The writer tells us that a good reputation is more valuable than wealth. A good name, and thus a good reputation, brings with it praise, influence, and prosperity. A good reputation excels other blessings in life. To be well thought of has more value than the temporary wealth of this world's riches.[50]

A person's reputation is important, especially in a town like ours. People will talk, and the word will spread quickly about what is going on and how people act in the community. To have the reputation this man/woman had is a true blessing from the Lord. His/her life was one of consistency and value that kept his/her reputation from being tarnished through the years.

---
50 Allen P. Ross, The Expositor's Bible Commentary, Volume 5, (Grand Rapids, Michigan: Zondervan Publishing House, 1991), 1059.

II. A True Blessing

"To be esteemed is better than silver or gold ..."

The word used here, "esteemed," means good favor. In other words, it is one well thought of and who has engaging qualities. The verse has a logical progression in that the first part really deals with people who know of someone; this part addresses those who actually knew the person. It is the difference between knowing about someone and actually knowing someone. To be this kind of person is to be blessed and to be a blessing to others[51] I know that you loved and appreciated this man/woman. You were blessed by him/her, and he/she was blessed by you and your friendship. This is a gift from God. In order to have friends, you must be a friend. He/she was a true friend.

Then there is a friend who is closer than anyone else we ever meet in this life: Jesus. This man/woman knew Jesus in his/her heart as his/her personal Savior. Because that is true, we can rest in the promises of Scripture: to be absent from the body is to be present with the Lord. We can also rejoice in the hope of a future reunion when all believers are gathered together in heaven with the Lord.

---

51 Ibid.

It is likely you will face the challenge of performing the funeral of someone killed in an accident. This is especially difficult when it involves a teenager. This outline came out of a situation where a fifteen-year-old was killed in a motorcycle accident one Sunday afternoon. He was a Christian, so I included assurance of his being in heaven with the Lord.

My God, Why?
Mark 15:33-34

I. Dark Day

We are told that darkness covered the land as Jesus hung dying on the cross from noon until 3:00 in the afternoon. Literally, it was a dark day. The darkness symbolized a great evil. It was a supernatural manifestation, not some strange physical phenomenon. It was during that time of darkness that all our sins were put on Jesus as He died for us. All the sins of humanity separated Jesus from His heavenly Father.[52]

Sunday was a dark day. There was news that none of us wanted to hear about this young man/woman. It was unthinkable, unbelievable, and hard to imagine. Our ears hear such news and we have a hard time accepting the reality of such a tragic event. I want you to remember that God was Lord over last Sunday, just like He is Lord over every day. Nothing caught Him off guard or by surprise. His presence and grace kept you through that day; it will keep you through today and every day you live.

---

52 James A. Brooks, The New American Commentary, Mark, (Nashville, Tennessee: Broadman Press, 1991), 260-261.

II. Desperate Cry

The Bible tells us that Jesus cried out to God the Father. He asked God why he had been forsaken. The Lord's cry shows us the depth of His suffering as He who knew no sin became sin for our salvation. Literally, the language implies that God left Jesus helpless in that moment. The moment had come for Jesus to pay the price for the sins of mankind, and He was drinking the bitter cup of death so we could live. God chose not to remove the bitter cup from Jesus and allowed His only Son to die for us on the cross.[53]

It is almost unimaginable to think about Jesus crying this out to God, yet we know that He did because our sins were upon Him, and those sins caused a separation between Jesus the Son and God the Father. Because Jesus died, forsaken on Calvary's hill, we can be forgiven through His grace.

III. Deliverance

We know from the other gospels that Jesus prayed, "Father, into Your hands I commit My spirit." Jesus went immediately into the presence of the Father when He breathed His last breath on the cross. God delivered Jesus from that horrible suffering called crucifixion. Jesus's death, burial, and resurrection deliver us from eternal death and punishment.[54]

This young man/woman has been delivered. To be absent from the body is to be present with the Lord. He/she is home with Jesus right now. One day, we who know Christ as Savior, will see him/her again. In the meantime, we must trust the Lord to help us through these days of hurt and sorrow.

---

53 Ibid.
54 Ibid.

The following outline came out of a situation in which a woman was diagnosed with cancer and died in her early sixties. In one of my visits with her, she contended that it was not her time to go. I gently reminded her of the truth of the Scriptures. God has a plan for all of us. There is a time to be born and a time to die. She was a strong believer in our church. I wanted to address the importance of knowing Jesus as Savior as the prerequisite to an eternity in heaven.

When Is It Time to Die?
Luke 2:25-32

Introduction

Whenever death comes for us, it is important to be ready. Regardless of the circumstances surrounding us, we can die in peace. When is it time to die? Simeon's life offers an example to consider.

Jesus was eight days old when His parents brought Him to the temple in Jerusalem and placed Him in the arms of an aged priest named Simeon to be dedicated to God. Simeon was a godly man who lived in expectancy of the coming Savior. The Holy Spirit had revealed to him in some way that he would not die until he had seen the Messiah.

I. When You Have a Passion For God (vv. 25–28)

Simeon was a good man. He was called just and devout. He lived in expectancy of the coming Messiah. He was in touch with and responsive to the Spirit of God. Christian people should live their lives in such a way that we won't be ashamed to face God. We should be faithful to God unto our death. When a person has lived faithfully, obediently, and with a passion for God, he or she can die in peace.[55]

This man/woman loved God, and God loved him/her. He/she lived his/her life with a passion for God. He/she sought to be right with the Lord. When he/she had issues in his/her life, he/she prayed about them and tried to be obedient to the Lord's leadership in his/her life. He/she had a passion for the Lord and His work.

II. When You Fulfill the Purpose of God (vv. 27–28)

Simeon is little known to us beyond this passage of Scripture. He enters the pages of the Bible for a brief moment, plays a part in the story of Jesus, and then exits, to be heard from no more. We don't know how, but the Holy Spirit told Simeon he would not die until he saw the Messiah. Simeon had Jesus placed in his arms at the temple that day. It was as if Simeon was born for this purpose, for this moment, and for this one act. Every child of God has a godly purpose to fulfill.[56]

---

[55] Norval Geldenhuys, The New International Commentary on the New Testament, Commentary on The Gospel of Mark, (Grand Rapids, Michigan: Wm. B. Eerdmans Publishing Company, 1983), 118-119.
[56] Ibid.

While Simeon seemingly had only one purpose to fulfill, I am sure there is more to his story. This dear one had a purpose in this life. God used him/her in some wonderful ways to minister to others. He/she was a good family member, church member, neighbor, and friend.

III. When You Have Made Preparation with God (vv. 29–32)

Simeon immediately acknowledged Jesus as Savior. He confessed his faith in Christ and described Him with glorious adoration. Simeon's life was complete because he met Jesus personally and accepted Him as the Lord and Savior of the world.[57]

This man/woman met the same Jesus personally. While he/she did not get to hold the baby Jesus in his/her arms, he/she did ask the risen Christ into his/her heart. When he/she died, this same Jesus welcomed him/her into His arms in heaven.

Conclusion

We don't understand everything life throws our way, but God does. He is still in control. While we would be tempted to argue that this one's life was far too short, we can be assured that God had a perfect plan for him/her.

---

57 Ibid.

Follow Up

In the chapter on my experience in Africa, I mentioned the tradition of the people going back to visit the grieving family in the third day after the funeral service. By comparison, our tradition tends to be that a great number of guests visit the bereaved before the funeral service, but few, if any, go back later.

Pastor, we need to change this tradition and do a better job of following up with grieving families. I will confess to you that I can do a better job of describing it than I do of performing it; however, I feel compelled to offer this challenge to everyone who ministers through funerals.

When there is a death in the community, especially the church community, people have a tendency to overwhelm the grieving family right away. People will make the time to call the family or go see them. Once the body is prepared at the funeral home, there is typically a steady stream of visitors. More often than not the bereaved family will receive enough food to feed ten times more people than they have in their entire clan. I cannot tell you how many people have told me they felt so guilty because of the amount of food they had to throw away because they could not eat it all before it spoiled. There will be cards, flowers, and hugs in abundance right up to the time of the funeral.

After the funeral, however, there is a noticeable drop off in the expressions of concern. There will be the obligatory questions and comments such as, "How are you doing?" or the ever-popular, "I am praying for you." As the family settles back into a routine following the funeral service for their loved one, the house can grow uncomfortably quiet. Flowers from the funeral begin to die, often serving as a painful reminder of their own loss. The phone rarely rings because most people fear they will "bother" the hurting family. While there is something to be said for private time during the grieving process, too much of it can be painful.

A wonderful strategy would be to schedule follow-up visits to grieving families, not unlike the follow up we do for those making decisions in church. The deacon body can be an invaluable tool at this point. Pastor, it would be wise for you to make a call on your church members after they have lost loved ones in death. It does not have to be a lengthy visit. A card from you can also be very effective in communicating genuine concern for a hurting family.

Someone has said that a person's grief is as unique and individual as the person's fingerprint. No two people go through the grieving process in exactly the same way. There will be those who take much longer than others. Some will hide pain behind a mask. Others will be embarrassed to talk about it, feeling that sadness is somehow equivalent to weakness. I find that the more difficult the death, the longer the process takes. The death of a child will change a parent forever. The sudden loss of someone special through an accident leaves an empty void in a family's life. Those who die senselessly at the hand of a criminal leave behind confusion as well as the pain of grief. One writer said that asking when grief is finished is like asking, "How high is up?" Pastor, the point is that you need to be available and willing to invest time in the people under your care who are hurting. When the phone has stopped ringing and the cards have stopped coming is when you will be needed most.

In addition to your ministry to the hurting ones in your congregation, you can give away a number of good books that are helpful. I suggest you lead your church to purchase a supply of these and have them available as gifts to the bereaved families of your community. I give away a good Christian book on grief and ask the person's permission to hear his/her opinion of the book. Such an approach does two things: it encourages the person to read the book, and it obligates me to do another follow-up visit. I have found this method helpful in finding the most meaningful books that do the most good. You will find a list of suggested resources at the end of this book.

I hope this work proves to be helpful. Ministry to grieving people can be some of the most difficult work but the most rewarding at the same time. If your own experience of grief brought you to this work, then I pray the comfort of the Father will bless you and keep you through your difficult journey. If you are being called upon to speak words of comfort to hurting people at a funeral service, then I pray God's wisdom and power will be upon you.

Suggested Resources

Experiencing Grief. H. Norman Wright. Nashville, Tennessee: Broadman & Holman, 2004.

Tracks of a Fellow Struggler. John Claypool. Waco, Texas: Word, 1974.

I'll Hold You in Heaven. Jack Hayford. Ventura, California: Regal Books, 1990.

Gone but Not Lost (Grieving the Death of a Child). David W. Wierbse. Grand Rapids, Michigan: Baker Book House, 1992.

It's Okay to Cry. H. Norman Wright. Colorado Springs, Colorado: WaterBrook Press, 2004.

Recovering from Losses in Life. H. Norman Wright. Grand Rapids, Michigan: Revell, 2006.